CHANCE
or CHOICE

Unlocking Innovation Success

CHANCE or CHOICE

Unlocking Innovation Success

Dr. Greg McLaughlin • Dr. Vinny Caraballo

CRC Press
Taylor & Francis Group
Boca Raton   London   New York

CRC Press is an imprint of the
Taylor & Francis Group, an **informa** business
A PRODUCTIVITY PRESS BOOK

CRC Press
Taylor & Francis Group
6000 Broken Sound Parkway NW, Suite 300
Boca Raton, FL 33487-2742

© 2013 by Taylor & Francis Group, LLC
CRC Press is an imprint of Taylor & Francis Group, an Informa business

No claim to original U.S. Government works

Printed in the United States of America on acid-free paper
Version Date: 20121107

International Standard Book Number: 978-1-4665-8186-9 (Paperback)

Library of Congress Cataloging-in-Publication Data

McLaughlin, Gregory C.
    Chance or choice : unlocking innovation success / Greg McLaughlin and Vinny Caraballo.
       pages cm
       Includes bibliographical references and index.
       ISBN 978-1-4665-8186-9
       1. Technological innovations--Management. 2. Diffusion of innovations. 3. New products. 4. Organizational change. I. Caraballo, Vinny. II. Title.

    HD45.M285 2013
    658.4'063--dc23   2012043467

Visit the Taylor & Francis Web site at
http://www.taylorandfrancis.com

and the CRC Press Web site at
http://www.crcpress.com

Contents

List of Illustrations

List of Tables

Preface

Over time, we (Dr. Greg McLaughlin and Dr. Vinny Caraballo) have developed an enduring interest in innovation. This section describes our personal and collective journeys in understanding the meaning of innovation.

As the architects of Project Impact (a research project that began this journey) and Global Targeting, Inc.'s ENOVALE® (the strategic approach proposed in this book), we approach innovation from two perspectives. Dr. Caraballo's background is in sales and marketing, whereas Dr. McLaughlin hails from the science and research and development (R&D) world. Our meeting makes one think of a popular Reese's peanut butter cup commercial where one individual eating a candy bar would bump into another with a jar of peanut butter, and they would mix their snacks. This led to an exchange of words between the two, "You stuck your chocolate in my peanut butter" or, from another perspective, "You got your peanut butter on my chocolate." This successful advertising campaign demonstrated how two potentially unrelated products combine to form a new product. It happened much the same for us. It was a chance encounter. For us, our involvement in academia brought us together; we shared an interest in trying to understand how product development and processes influenced sales and marketing.

When we first met, we were both teaching courses at the graduate level. Our common bond or alignment is that we had both received our doctorate in business administration from Nova Southeastern University. We took pride in being consultants who were able to convert scholarly and academic work, turning it into practical solutions valued by our clients. Greg already had significant experience in the world of product development and science. He was heavily involved in Six Sigma and quality improvement, as well as working with R&D organizations.

Greg's interest in innovation comes from the many years he consulted on quality improvement and Six Sigma projects. Many of these projects were true innovations, rather than improvements, and netted many hundreds of millions of dollars of sustained profit. Greg had spent a great deal of time consulting and assisting with research and development projects, even writing a book on how to implement quality improvement in R&D. This led him to understand that innovation was more than just new products or technologies. He spent much of his working career helping companies, organizations, and governmental agencies to improve or change what they did. This set the stage for his interest in innovation and the chance encounter with Vinny.

Vinny's early interest in understanding innovation began with his career at IBM. In the early 1990s, IBM introduced the OS2 operating system to compete with Microsoft Windows. This was the application of mainframe technology to the PC. So why did IBM not dominate this market? This question was puzzling for years, as Vinny initially believed that the product was ahead of the market. Nevertheless, how could IBM have missed the mark? Was Microsoft just better at marketing? Was OS2 not as good as people had thought? Was the sales force led to believe this? Was IBM somehow less than serious about creating a PC operating system in the early 1990s? After all, one of the customer engineers did mention that one should "never trust a computer you can pick up." This thought led Vinny to a series of very good questions and, eventually, to a doctoral dissertation in a related field.

The Need for Research

There was a need to understand the role of innovation in an organization, given that most innovations involved only improving or developing new technologies—that is, how corporations or businesses implemented innovation and the connection between R&D and marketing. For the technology sector, there was a need to understand the special relationship between R&D and Marketing. The dominant themes of this R&D–Marketing interface were topics such as organizational R&D budgets, patents, science and technology, and how firms in the industry used this to their advantage. Greg was already working in the field, in multiple industries. As Vinny did research in the area, studied the literature, and studied different companies, he kept seeing a common thread of terms that were relevant to the R&D–Marketing interface. Some of these included *entrepreneurship, intrapreneurship, grassroots initiatives, championing, product development,* and *innovation.*

Except when new technology was explained or described, innovation in the 1990s was not a well defined term. Instead, management consultants focused more on processes. Innovation was a term associated with technology and science. Although Vinny was in the technology industry, his perspective was that of a marketer and remains so today. Eventually, he conducted his research with an emphasis on improving information flows between R&D and Marketing as a way to improve product development efforts in corporations What he did not realize is that this research had the most potential in the emerging field of innovation.

As technological capabilities began improving and proliferating through the Internet and opportunities for conducting business on a global scale increased, so did the places from where work in the IT industry could be delivered and parsed out. Cost reduction was the first driver for seeking new delivery destinations. Eventually, delivering work on a cost advantage basis became less of a benefit because many providers could deliver similar results. Companies could achieve lasting success through competitive advantage. Vinny witnessed this firsthand as he attended different outsourcing and offshoring meetings.

When you begin a research effort, it is often difficult to find the organizations that are best suited to support your efforts and are willing to do so, especially if you are just trying to make your name in the field. These entities are protective of their constituencies and always want to receive some sort of benefit for using their mailing lists. However, this provided Vinny with a valuable lesson.

Always go back to those organizations that have supported you in the past because you were also there for them when they needed you. This was the case for Vinny with the Hispanic Alliance for Career Enhancement (HACE).

HACE is a nonprofit corporation that has a mission of helping young Latinos develop and expand their professional careers. Vinny was a beneficiary of their services when he chose to change careers. Vinny had spent 11 years as an aviator in the U.S. Army, and after being stationed in Chicago, he chose to leave the service. It was through HACE that IBM hired Vinny. He later served on the HACE board and eventually as chair of the organization. Consequently, he still has a great deal of loyalty to the organization and still has a vested interest in its success. Vinny had remained close to the organization, so when he asked their help to distribute the survey, they were happy to comply. The participation in this study was exceptional. He was surprised at how large the participation was and how HACE was interested in the results for its constituents. Vinny now had a large sample that could provide enough data to do some meaningful analysis. This paved the way for us to extend the research to other demographic groups in the United States and the rest of the world.

Vinny sat on these numbers for a while, not really doing much with them. He was continuing to build his networks from around the world. While attending the Academy of Management in Montreal, he sat in on a session on

Latin America with a small group of professors from the region. As they all took their turn speaking, one could hear their Spanish accents in most of the group members, but there was one person in particular that had a unique accent, one that Vinny had never heard before. It was Dr. Carmen Joham of the University of South Australia. It was the first time that Vinny heard an Aussie with a Spanish accent. Carmen was originally from Venezuela, but had become a citizen of Australia.

The two had the time to get to know each other at the event while Vinny spoke at the conference on his research. She was interested in hearing more and for Vinny to meet her colleague Dr. Stephen Boyle. Thus, we decided to begin collaborating, and our first global partnership emerged.

An enthusiastic Australian team jumped into the research and has remained committed to the effort to this day. They also added a leadership dimension to the work. They began distributing the survey in Australia and later expanded it to Hong Kong, Indonesia, and Malaysia. Shortly after this meeting, we were joined by Professor Leonardo Pinedas of Universidad del Rosario in Bogota, Colombia. Given the poor response rate of the first survey distribution in South America, Vinny quickly rectified the problem. Through his connections, we went back, uncovered additional resources, and were able to add significant numbers to data sets.

Third Time Is the Charm

How to handle this data set became the primary question. This is where Greg appeared. Vinny had spoken to him about the work he was doing in innovation, and Greg was interested in learning more. However, Vinny guessed the true appeal was the large size of the sample. It quickly became obvious to him that, any time you have a large amount of data, someone that has a statistics background will always have an interest. Analyzing the data was something that Greg promised to do.

He simply said, "I'll analyze it for you," and has remained at the forefront of developing proprietary information for Project Impact and Global Targeting, Inc.

It took three attempts to get Greg's interest. In his first attempt, Vinny simply explained what he was doing in innovation. Greg seemed politely interested, but was not sure what Vinny wanted to do with the analysis. The second time we talked about the research project was during a conference call with the Australian team and a Malaysian collaborator. Greg still was not sure why he was on the call. Then he shared the data analysis, and you could see the excitement of trying to uncover the value in the analysis. Greg went to work on the analysis, validated the research, and created a methodology for innovation success. The rest, as they say, is history.

Acknowledgments

I, Dr. Gregory McLaughlin, would like to acknowledge all those who helped me over the years to create and hone this innovation philosophy. This includes the many companies I worked for, the many wonderful people I worked with, and the opportunity to learn and expand my skills.

I would especially like to thank my dear wife, Heidi, who has freely given of her wisdom, advice, and counsel concerning this book. Without her patience and love, this book would not be possible.

This book is a combination of knowledge and experience that requires effort and sacrifice. It is made possible because I, Dr. Vinny Caraballo, had the support of those individuals that sacrificed their time and resources for me. Thus, I dedicate this book to Ada, Ervin, Michelle, and my late parents, Ervin and Yolanda, for all they have done for me.

Chapter 1

The Innovation Conundrum

Background

In the twenty-first century, advances in technology, transportation, and new business models have enabled companies of all sizes to operate on a global scale. This globalization of business allows companies to enter new markets once thought the exclusive domain of the giant enterprises. Consequently, the bigger or more established firms find themselves looking to differentiate themselves from new competitors. In this environment, innovation has emerged as that competitive differentiator that will help companies establish themselves as global leaders. Innovation is certainly not a new concept in the information and technology age, but it has been generally restricted to the research and development (R&D) domain. As we move deeper into a knowledge-based economy that leverages robust informational infrastructures, innovation is presented with a more resounding and diversified voice. You now hear the word "innovation" in advertising to consumer markets, and in internal corporate communications, and even in daily conversation with the intent to leverage the word to signify success.

This increased frequency and emphasis on innovation has elevated the term to a "rock star" status in management vernacular.

As the term continues its path toward becoming ubiquitous, it also becomes a confusing concept to business professionals trying to develop growth-oriented programs for their companies. Companies and organizations understand its importance for further growth and competitiveness. The question is how first to implement and then facilitate ongoing (recurring) innovation. Executives and leaders seem to think that innovation occurs by chance rather than by choice. They search for a great idea that will provide a distinctive competitive advantage. Some organizations create an entire department to focus their energies on developing the next best technology or product. However, when examined from a strategic perspective, innovation projects occur on an infrequent basis, more due to "luck" than true planning. Although there is a goal to be innovative, there seems to be little or no strategy that directs the organization to internalize innovation.

The Innovation Conundrum

As we watched innovation go from the science and technology realm into the marketing and product development arena, the term innovation defined the advertisement more than the product itself. Consider Nissan's "Innovation for the planet, and innovation for all" campaign, as of this writing. What exactly does this mean? How can innovation be for all? Is it more about the technology? Alternatively, does the word innovation truly have any specific meaning, given its overuse? The popular use of the word seems to indicate that it is a descriptor of a new or novel (unique) product that has a high-tech component or application.

Given its popularity, academics and the scholar community also took an interest in understanding the concept of innovation. They studied companies, processes, and successes, and they developed theories and concepts to explain and understand innovation. The problem was that innovation seemed to be associated only with technology. If there was no technological outcome, then was there any innovation associated with it? Innovation almost became the exclusive domain of the technology companies. Given this emphasis on technology, other nontechnical products, services, and processes could not be truly innovative. Scholars along with their management counterparts attempted to broaden innovation's sphere of influence. Creativity became an initiator of innovation and moved innovation efforts beyond technology. Applying creative tools and techniques to a solution was deemed "innovative." From this came a host of new techniques and methods.

"Thought leaders" developed concepts such as open innovation, disruptive innovation, and blue ocean strategies. Many companies experienced success with these processes. Fundamentally, these processes present a method for moving new products or technology to completion by leapfrogging the competition. These processes bring forward another challenge to innovation: Just like technology seemed to be driving innovation, the idea of a process or methodology seemed more important than the innovation outcome that companies were looking to develop. The focus shifted to the process applied rather than the outcome desired. Moving from the outcome to the process, the strategies become process focused rather than organizationally applicable. What was missing was a central strategy for implementing innovation in any department. These processes and techniques provided a method to take an existing new product or technology and bring it more quickly to market. What was missing was how to initiate a successful innovation on a recurring basis.

Open innovation is perhaps the biggest culprit of focusing excessively on processes and not the individual. This concept is based on sharing and distributing knowledge with networks. It emphasizes openness, but is this appropriate for all organizations? There are multiple sites and forums established to share best practices in innovation. To practitioners, the infrastructure and establishing networks seem to be the driving forces. At some point, managing the networks becomes so complicated that much of the work is difficult to access. The questions become, "How do we manage the network to get to the best practices?" "Whom should we bring into the network?" Of course, there is the proprietary nature of some institutions that gain competitive advantages by not sharing. Additionally, many of these "open innovation" forums also have their own agendas. Essentially, it becomes about the group and not the innovator.

Disruptive innovation presents the opportunity for an interesting discussion. Is this a proactive methodology or a study in history? It appears that most of what one reads describes what happened. Leaders and managers need a strategy, not just a process or methodology. Forward thinking individuals need to focus beyond the process to the eventual outcome. It seems that many of these new innovation techniques are more process oriented than results oriented. Where is the human element in all this? Who determines if something is actually innovative? Is that not where the beliefs of individuals come into play? How do you pick any of those processes when they may not fit the definition or profile of your workforce, customers, or infrastructure?

Internally (within the organization), leaders search for methods and practices that ensure success. What works for one type of innovation is not feasible (repeatable) with a different project. Add to this the global aspects of business that product life cycles are becoming shorter. There is a need for finding an innovation strategy that delivers measurable results. This search continues today with most leaders searching for the "holy grail."

As you embark on this journey to understand innovation, we want you to read this book with the intention of taking away three points that drove our research:

- Innovation emanates from human beings.
- We have simplified a complex concept through definitional clarity.

■ Innovation success can be achieved through ENOVALE®
Solutions.

Throughout the book, we will provide you with tools and
concepts that you can implement in your organizations to help
you move from just surviving a brutally competitive landscape,
filled with new and diversified competitors, to leading your
teams in leveraging innovative capabilities valued by your customers and users. What makes this endeavor different is that
our work originates from research, experience, and empirical evidence. Opinions, feelings, and emotions have no basis
in fact and therefore are merely conjecture. Our research
results have value because you can apply them. The results
come from our work in Project Impact, an ongoing multiyear
global study to measure attitudes, opinions, and disposition
of different cultures towards innovation.

Project Impact

Competing messages and interpretation of innovation, cou-
pled with confusing processes and definitions, finally got us
to the point of asking, "What does innovation really mean?"
We began our search to give meaning to innovation and we
launched "Project Impact." At first, this had no name. It was
just our study on innovation. The name came afterward. We
were explaining this to so many people that we had to shorten
the description. In one of his conversations, Vinny remembered
mentioning that this study would measure how culture impacts
innovation; thus, the name of this research project emerged.

Most corporations and organizations have a global workforce that adds complexity to finding and implementing
a single, cohesive innovation strategy. This confusion and
indecisiveness encouraged Dr. Vinny Caraballo to investigate
innovation from a research perspective. Project Impact, with
its goal to understand what innovation means to those who
use it, was born out of this decision.

The South American software industry served as the first test location for this research. Selecting this region had advantages because it had just begun to surface as a destination of choice for the outsourcing industry. It is in the same time zone as the United States and labor is delivered at a reasonable cost. We believed that if the region were to become relevant to, say, the outsourcing industry and compete against the rest of the world, it would be important to understand the disposition of its residents toward innovation. This also established the first principle of the study: *global in scale.* South America was also a logical starting point because Vinny was teaching at a Peruvian university and was witnessing the investment the region was making in higher education. It also helped that one of his students was the owner of a health-care software developer and head of the Peruvian Software Development Association. This gave us access to the industry leaders in the country.

After distributing the survey, Vinny was disappointed with the small number of completed surveys. There was little to analyze, and this kept him searching to find organizations with a large number of members to survey. He continued his focus on South America, and it occurred to him that what he was looking for was culture—not necessarily country of origin. After all, is it not a reality that a country can have multiple cultures within its borders? As people become more mobile and immigration patterns change, they bring their beliefs and customs with them and make adjustments to adapt to new surroundings. Was that not true with Latinos in the United States? Has this culture in the United States influenced society? Of course it has. Then why not understand this demographic's inclination toward innovation? The U.S. Latino population became the culture of interest.

For the United States, the fastest growing segments are those individuals who can trace their roots to Spanish-speaking countries in Latin America (Central and South America and the Caribbean area). This group is frequently referred to as Latinos or Hispanics. In the twentieth century, all of these countries were classified as less developed or "Third World" nations. Their close proximity to the United States presented an opportunity for immigration to the United States. These individuals brought with them their cultural beliefs.

It was not enough to look at an overall perspective; Project Impact also examined demographic effects (gender differences, differences between job functions and generational cohorts) so as to learn how best to interpret multicultural innovation. To begin, we chose a relatively homogenous group of individuals with multiple industries. We wanted a group that had experience with frequent innovations with short life cycles. Individuals from a Latino or Hispanic background working within the IT industry became the test group. This group is unique since it shares a large number of common attributes. The group was easily identifiable within the United States.

The results were an eye-opener that radically changed our perspective of innovation. There were no differences between males and females for the group studied. There were differences between job function and generational cohorts when comparing the meaning of innovation. Project Impact went further than just demographics as the results led us to the realization that, to understand innovation, one would have to understand it from an individual perspective. Thus, we focused on delivering the findings of Project Impact in a simplified manner that can help in managing innovation on a daily basis in your organizations—that is, weaving innovation into the organizational fabric of corporate and governmental agencies.

Our proprietary ENOVALE methodology has its beginnings in Project Impact. Project Impact began as a way for us to understand how people define innovation, and how they value it. Everywhere that we travel, people define innovation differently. For some, an innovation is the creation of something new, whereas for others an innovation can be copying and improving something that already exists. Essentially, there is no universally accepted understanding of innovation. However, there are definitions in dictionaries and encyclopedias, and some organizations have published their perspective on the topic.

In our research, we found as many as 60 different definitions describing innovation. Project Impact searched for a more refined definition of innovation that could better describe what innovation accomplished. Thus, the dilemma was: How do people understand innovation? Trying to decipher how people understand innovation was an excellent place to start. This was the starting point of Project Impact and the fascinating results that this research has produced to date.

In the beginning of Project Impact, it was important to stay guided by its founding principles. First, it had to be global in scale. If our initial hypothesis was that people from a diverse cultural background think of innovation differently, then we had to seek out different cultures to get an understanding and to provide some definitional clarity. Therefore, we established a plan to survey major cultural groups.

This endeavor began like most social research in that it looked to answer a question: Given that innovation is a key ingredient for success, is there a simple but effective method of understanding innovation from an individual perspective? The best approach was to do an empirically based study that would provide enough evidence so that we could form a concept based on facts—that is, analyzing data that would answer our research questions. This led us to the work of Zhuang (1995) and Zhuang, Williamson, and Carter (1999), who produced a survey instrument that we found usable. We choose the instrument for its ability to measure how individuals understand the meaning of innovation. We found Zhuang's instrument valuable, but one that was never exploited to its full potential. It appears that the data it produced were capable of delivering a more meaningful application or solution. We modified the instrument with additional demographic questions (gender, age, job position, education, etc.) and questions related to how individuals value innovation. In addition, we added questions as to which groups contribute to and lead innovation efforts best.

The second guiding principle of Project Impact is that results are *empirically driven*. Choosing a quantitative, nonexperimental method by administering a survey provided information needed for statistical analysis. The results clarified what our respondents were telling us: Innovation is best understood from the individual. This led to some interesting findings that became the basis for many of the models we developed.

From our research, innovation was too often associated with non-evidence-based opinion or perhaps a single, isolated occurrence of an event. Essentially, for this work to be acceptable as a valid effort to understand how different people define innovation, we had to have good scholarly and academic justification. From an overall perspective of the innovation data collected, there were four major topics. Applying sophisticated statistical software enabled us to identify them: problem framing, novelty and utility, ambition level, and creative destruction. With the help of innovation strategist Tony Bynum, we applied design thinking and produced the innovation value model (IVM), shown in Figure 1.1.

Topics	Defining Elements of Innovation			
Cognition & Modalities	**Abstract:** requires the ability to think in an abstract and conceptual manner.		**Concrete:** the ability to make sense of current conditions and take action based on measurable and empirical evidence.	
Factors & Drivers	**Intrinsic Factors:** factors or considerations that inform or define the innovation itself (the DNA of the innovation).		**Extrinsic Factors:** outside or external factors that describe, define or profile the conditions that inform innovation (the conditions in which the innovation lives)	
Principles	**Problem Framing**	**Novelty & Utility**	**Ambition Level**	**Creative Destruction** (continuous improvement)
	The act of reframing current conditions based on the PESTEL forces impacting the environment.	The ability to conceive and deliver solutions that are distinct and deliver newly recognized value to the market or end user(s).	An observable (quantifiable) propensity towards risk.	The ability and belief in regular and proactive obsolescence of one's existing solutions in an effort to outpace competitive threats.

Spectrum →

Figure 1.1   Innovation value model. (Source: Caraballo, Bynum, and McLaughlin, 2012).

The IVM is helpful in location-based decisions. It helps managers decide if certain cultures are more predisposed to create or improve. It is a useful tool when used at the macro level. As we continued to drill deeper into the data, we found that we could define innovation at the "atomic" level. That is, we could identify how individuals define what innovation means to them personally.

Finally, Project Impact needed to be *application oriented*. It needed to have sustained benefits for business managers who want to solve their innovation problems. This became the third principle.

Consequently, we piloted Global Targeting, Inc.'s innovation solution strategy with Choucair Testing, a Colombia-based software testing outsourcer. This company was ideal because its founder (a true innovator) had identified a need in the country's IT industry and developed a business around that need. Eventually, the company grew from a start-up with informal processes to a medium size organization requiring more sophisticated management techniques. Its organization represents the complexities of a modern business needing to innovative to compete globally. There were challenges in processes, objectives, and communications. Achieving innovation success on a regular basis had become more difficult. Increased competition was providing more pressure for this company to differentiate itself. Consequently, the experience we gained through this venture helped us validate our methodology through an engagement that delivered measurable value.

Globalization Drives Innovation

With increasing globalization, the need to understand innovation from an individual perspective becomes all that more important. One such element of globalization is that of outsourcing and offshoring. Toward the beginning of the twenty-first century, outsourcing and offshoring became more attractive alternatives for companies to achieve cost savings. This created a surge in destination development and a race to find the next best place to outsource. No developed country wanted to miss the opportunity, but less-developed countries saw in it the advantage to compete based on developing intellectual capital and skills with a cost-effective business model—that is, delivering services, products, or technology based on lower cost.

India became the first dominant player and remains in that position today due to its size and proclivity to produce engineering graduates. China, the Philippines, Vietnam, and a variety of others followed with a claim of pricing competitiveness; this was followed by a third wave in Latin America and Eastern Europe. This led to globalization and a model based on delivering services around the clock. Any time zone became the mantra of competitiveness. However, after most companies had achieved a presence in multiple geographies, value became the operative term. Value was essentially a "what you get is what you paid for" term. This certainly appears to be a part of the outsourcing business model, but availability of global talent combined with competitive pricing seems to put everyone competing on scale. This is where leveraging innovation presented an opportunity for companies to differentiate themselves.

The Final Step

The third principle brings together Project Impact and Global Targeting, Inc.'s ENOVALE Solutions. Project Impact and ENOVALE Solutions became a reality because they combine new thinking on a global perspective. Everything begins and ends with the efforts of the individual. The "IN" in the word innovation is also the first two letters of the word INdividual. Achieving innovation success requires the unique perspective of individuals aligned to project objectives.

What started as a global quantitative research project now needed application in the real world. Global Targeting, Inc. developed ENOVALE Solutions as a corporate or organization strategy with a design to reality (successful project) structure. Since we had gone from a cultural view down to the individual level of defining innovation, we could now identify the selection of individuals with the right alignment for a successful innovation outcome. We committed to defining innovation at the individual level as well as refining the strategy to show that it is valuable in helping companies and organizations institutionalize innovation.

The remainder of this book is dedicated to the mechanics for implementing ENOVALE in your organizations. Thus, we are able to share our end-to-end experience with you with the intent that it will make your innovation journey much more productive. Our experiences have shown us that the development of this strategy began as a problem needing a solution and ended with a solution: ENOVALE Solutions solving a problem.

Summary

The purpose of this book is to provide a "how to" approach to implementing an innovation strategy that applies throughout an organization or business. No longer limited to Research and Development or Engineering Departments, innovation can occur in any department or within any function. Our research has shown us that innovation begins with the individual and therefore the individual is the ultimate innovator in the corporation or business. We provide strong support for our ideas, as these are generally not the topics found in most innovation texts. Rather than just talking about our ideas, we provide tools and techniques for implementation. Our approach is to use validated research data and convert them into practical applications.

This book is intentionally short so that you can read this on a flight of two hours or more. We do not burden you with the scholarly research but condense this into practical information ready for implementation. The information contained within is also a compilation of 60 years' worth of experience and common sense, something obviously lost in many corporate endeavors.

The remaining chapters describe and explain the ENOVALE Solutions strategy. It is the product of Global Targeting, Inc., based on the ongoing research of Project Impact—a global study to measure attitudes, opinions, and disposition of different cultures toward innovation. We confirm that it shows how a global collaborative effort can provide sound and practical solutions to solving innovation management problems.

Beginning with Chapter 2, which provides more evidence for developing an innovation strategy, Chapters 3 through 11 explain each element of ENOVALE and Chapter 12 discusses a project strategy useful for any type of innovation planned. Let us know your thoughts and how you plan to implement this innovation strategy. Go to the website for Global Targeting, Inc. (www.globaltargeting.com) to leave your comments or questions.

Chapter 2

Individuals and Innovation

Defining How Individuals Perceive Innovation

The problem lies in the fact that the word innovation means many different things to many different people. If you research the word in the dictionary, you will find that the most common definition uses two key words: "new" or "novel."

An innovation is a new idea or novel (unique) concept. Global Targeting, Inc. uses this definition and expands on its meaning. Inventions are certainly innovations. They change our lives; they transform the way we do things; they shift the boundaries of our knowledge. The U.S. Patent Office receives numerous applications each day to protect inventions, but to most people these innovations are unique and special—not something thought of as ordinary. Inventions occur irregularly and often by chance rather than with a concerted effort. They are truly special events that are not often repeated or replicated. For many, the "holy grail" for continuous innovation is a strategy that imitates and sustains innovation on a regular basis. That strategy would not restrict innovations only to "new" items but would also include innovations that improve products, services, and technology. In fact, the term could easily apply to people and decisions that have resulted in a positive outcome. That is, innovation has a much broader definition than that which is often applied to it.

Baregheh, Rowley, and Sambrook (2009) found more than 60 individual definitions of the word innovation. We know the word means many things to different people. Some see innovation as a novel idea; yet, ideas are creative but not innovative, given their intangibility. In reality, innovation is more than new ideas; it is new technology, new ways of operating, and new ways of managing. Innovation occurs when humans employ a creative process to meet a particular need; innovation begins at a very human level. You could even call this the "organic" level. Therefore, a correct definition should include the contribution of human beings to address a need with available resources. Innovation begins at the human level, with creative thought and a reason to fulfill an important need. A single word or group of words cannot adequately describe or define innovation on an individual basis.

From our study and empirical research, we arrived at a definition that describes innovation from a perspective of what the innovation will accomplish. This will help clarify how individuals perceive (understand) innovation. People encounter products, services, and new technology and can easily define these as innovative if they either meet a new need or better address an existing need. Individuals use their knowledge and experience to determine innovativeness. Our experiences tell us when something is better, especially when that object meets or exceeds our needs. We judge this object as innovative when it better meets our needs.

In order to clarify a definition of innovation that will relate to an individual's understanding, Baregheh et al. (2009) decided to examine the "means of innovation" (p. 1334)—that is, understanding how innovation "transforms ideas into new, improved or changed" (p. 1334) items, services, or people. From this definition and our research, we arrived at three unique descriptors of innovation that transform objects to meet new or different needs.

We use three descriptive words to define how innovation transforms objects. The three main descriptors or themes are new, improved, or change that describes how the product, technology, or service is transformed—in other words, how the product, service, or technology is "transformed" into something we define as innovative as it better meets our needs. There is a distinctive strategy for each of the three descriptors. This makes sense, since most leaders and managers are interested in innovation from a perspective of what it will accomplish or, as we say, "the outcome produced." When customers or users experience a product, service, or technology designed to exceed more than what they expect, then we identify this as true innovation. As expectations change, so do our needs.

Congratulate yourself if you felt that the meaning of innovation was something more than an invention! You are the best judge of whether something is innovative or not. Where our meaning differs from others is that innovation is more than something that is new. It is more than a creative idea or new technology: It is a means to meet a need (new or existing) with something better than presently exists.

Think about the Apple® iPad (version 4 as of this writing). Is this innovative? Well, if we used the standard terms of innovation we would ask whether it is a new technology or new to the marketplace. Is it a repackage of the Tablet PC or a new update? Whatever you believe it to be, it is innovative as it specifically addresses a need. We define innovation from its ability to meet a human need. The fact is that the iPad is innovative without being very new (obviously, it has some new hardware or software or technology) or novel. Consider a second piece of technology: the cell phone. Is the cell phone truly new or novel or an improvement on existing technology? Given that the cell phone became popular beginning in 1990, is the cell phone today truly something new or unique or, rather, quite an improvement over its 1990 predecessor?

We believe that most people will say that their cell phones today are an improvement over what existed previously. That being the case, the cell phone of today is innovative as it fulfills many needs as compared to its 1990 predecessor. Innovation occurs numerous times when improvements or changes occur to an existing technology, product, or service.

Defining the "Means" of Innovation

As mentioned previously, innovation consists of three distinct themes, concepts, or categories. Each concept or theme describes the innovation transformation. The innovation (its definition individualized) transforms into three distinctive themes or dimensions. Think of these as three distinctive methods or ways of accomplishing the same goal, innovation. For example, consider that stocks, bonds, or commodities are methods or ways to invest money. All accomplish the same goal (hopefully), classified by type of investment. Each investment type requires a unique (and often related) strategy. Innovation follows the same pattern.

Theme 1: **new** (something new or a novel [unique] idea; an invention)—normally, we think of new technology.

Theme 2: **improvement** (making something better)—this relates to products, processes, or services. Improvement is for those products, processes, or services that are underperforming.

Theme 3: **change** (changes in products, processes, services, technology, and people resulting in a positive outcome). Change affects people the most—both physically and emotionally. Innovative change is a positive change with a tangible benefit.

Each theme is distinctive, yet interrelated as all need the individual to initiate and recognize the innovation. What is different is how individuals perceive their importance. Of all three themes, innovative change is not widely acknowledged. This is probably the most overlooked aspect of innovation. We believe this is where Global Targeting, Inc. has its greatest opportunity. Making change positive is truly innovative as it directly affects us all. Surprisingly, people frequently recognize it as being the most important and significant theme (descriptor) of innovation. Think back to when change occurred in your job, your boss, or your life. Was it positive? Did it make a difference? Did it change you for the better? If it did, it was innovative.

Of course, a negative experience may have also changed you. If the change was positive, then the outcome was innovative. A negative experience could easily lead to a negative outcome that defines destructive change. Negative experiences can also result from destructive change—change made with a negative intent. Many times the situation warrants a negative outcome, but the process, the communications, and the repercussions can lead to destructive change. Destructive changes affect morale, motivation, and productivity issues. These are anti-innovative with consequences and repercussions that may be devastating. The positive and innovative aspects of change will become a topic of discussion later in this book.

Each theme or transformation continuously defines what the innovation will accomplish. When we "define" innovation, we use these terms—not as a definition but more as a descriptor of what the innovation will accomplish. If the item satisfies unfulfilled or "new" needs, it is innovative. If the need is for an improvement of what exists, then that is innovation. There will never be a time when a group of individuals can all agree on a single definition of innovation; however, when the object fills or meets a need, then they can agree that what transformed it was innovative. Whether you recognize the item or the transformation, you will be able to distinguish the three dimensions of innovation.

The exciting element of the last statement was that the transformation could be innovative. For organizations or businesses searching for innovation, we have found you a function for innovation. Innovation is not a special event, a chance encounter, an unexpected discovery. You do not wait for the next invention; you take what you have and make it better. This may seem to go against what you have believed—and it does. Rather than be beholden to pure luck, you have a choice to decide how to apply the innovative skills of the organization to which products, services, processes, or technology. Remember that innovation begins and ends with the individual. If we experience something better than expected and it meets more of our needs, then we say it is innovative. Innovativeness increases as the organization meets more needs of the customer or user.

Without getting into detailed specifics, we have scientifically validated these three themes (means) of innovation with numerous cultural and ethnic groups worldwide, through the work of Project Impact. What is interesting is that each cultural group identifies the three themes; however, the strongest theme varies from group to group (culture to culture). Using the research data identified through Project Impact, we were able to see distinctive patterns when we grouped the data by three distinct demographic categories (gender, generation, and job function). Each of the groups identified the three innovation themes but applied a different importance (strength) rating to each theme. Figure 2.1 details the results of the Project Impact Study.

The results, which originate from a comprehensive survey, indicate that no significant differences exist between genders but differences do exist between generations and job functions. Technical individuals tended to understand innovation very differently than nontechnical individuals. Technical individuals placed a higher priority on the new dimension of innovation; nontechnical placed more priority on change and improvements. Even more significant was the difference

Demographic characteristics			Strength factor		
			1	2	3
Millenial	Tech	M	Actively improve	New perspectives	Follows the leader
Millenial	Tech	F	Change	Improve	New
Millenial	Nontech	M	Improve	Change	New
Millenial	Nontech	F	Change	New	Improve
Gen X	Tech	M	Improve	Change	New perspectives
Gen X	Tech	F	Change/improve	Follows the leader	New perspectives
Gen X	Nontech	M	Change	Improve	New
Gen X	Nontech	F	Change	Improve	New
Baby Boom	Tech	M	Change	New	Improve
Baby Boom	Tech	F	Change	Improve	New
Baby Boom	Nontech	M	Change	New	Improve
Baby Boom	Nontech	F	Actively improve	Change	New

Figure 2.1   Alignment matrix. (Source: Caraballo and McLaughlin, 2012).

between three generations (Millennials, born between 1980 and 1998; Generation X, born between 1964 and 1979; and the Baby Boom generation, born between 1946 and 1964). These generations take a very different view of innovation by applying a unique priority ranking to the three themes.

These results and those for many different cultural or ethnic groups validate the three-dimensional nature of innovation. The results also confirm that innovation originates from the individual, although certain demographic groups do share similar characteristics. What varies from one cultural group to another is the strength of the theme that is most prominent. In addition, the proprietary survey provides information on how individuals perceive their work environment, what they value, and what they need to be innovative. This information provides those who supply products, technology, and services a unique competitive advantage. Global Targeting, Inc. offers this detailed analysis to all of our clients.

When presented to senior management, there is a profile of how the organization views innovation. These results could lead to a potential conflict, given how individuals understand innovation. There is nothing more compelling than asking an individual to define the word innovation and listening to the various definitions that both complement and conflict with each other. Various conflicting definitions, as expressed by their employees, have shocked many of those in authority. Given the diversity of opinion, it is easy to understand how conflict, dissent, and disengagement cripple the chances for success.

Influencing Perceptions of Innovation

We all perceive innovation in our own ways. We use knowledge and experience of products, services, and technology to determine if we designate the object as innovative. Once we build up enough information about an object, we can judge any changes that occur and, from that standard, determine whether those changes are innovative. It is important to recognize that we use our knowledge and experience to identify innovation. Needs drive the innovation but our use of and experience with a product hone and refine our knowledge. The more we experience a product, service, or process, the better we can understand its performance and determine the degree of innovativeness. Sometimes only a minor improvement is innovative—as long as we meet our needs. We also know that individuals identify improvement when the need is met in a realistic time frame. It is best to understand that people will perceive something as innovative because it exceeds the performance of something with which they are experienced.

Obviously, from a business perspective, we cannot know what each person perceives as innovative and we do not need to know this. What we can do is to determine the amount of transformation that a product, service, or technology requires in order for a majority of people to recognize it as innovative. Knowing this gives the firm a competitive advantage.

A transformation can take many forms. It can be a very new technology, a vastly improved product, or a significant change to personnel or process. Companies and organizations that transform their offerings without first considering their customer (user) needs will most often fail. It is not enough to "make something better"; it requires the product, technology, process, or service to meet more than existing needs. Customers respond (by purchasing) when their needs are better met. Meeting new needs or refining needs met previously can accomplish the same objective. The "trick" is finding the balance between meeting needs and determining the amount of transformation that an object requires. Knowing what to transform offers the business or organization real competitive advantage.

For new products, services, or technologies, business leaders often begin with a small group of innovators who will familiarize people with a new or improved product. A perfect example of this is the Apple iPad, which essentially replaced the tablet PC. What made the iPad innovative was that it met more needs than its predecessor. This is why we say that when you increase the need you also increase those who purchase. For the Apple iPad, it was a small group of so-called pioneers that invested in the iPad. When they experienced more of their needs being met (such as size, weight, function, etc.), they proclaimed the iPad as a new innovation. The pioneers "transformed" perceptions of what a product such as the iPad could accomplish and specifically how it met more needs. Many times communications, marketing, and advertising favorably transform perceptions. However, unless needs are better met or distinctly new, an offering will not be perceived as innovative. Transforming perceptions is not enough: The physical product, process, technology, or service must perform.

What if the communications do not discuss or even hint at innovation? Only some of the public will get the message, but the opportunity is lost. This could give competition amble time to respond with an inferior product that appears to meet more needs. We have numerous examples of stories such as these where the leader subjugates his or her authority to a well informed organization that appears to be the innovative player. This is the specific reason that innovation cannot be purely chance or unexpected discoveries.

Innovation is not just about meeting or exceeding needs, but also about exceeding performance. At times, we will find that people will identify innovation as purely performance driven because the object meets all critical needs. We cannot know what everyone is thinking, but we do know that when people see an object that meets their needs, they can identify it as innovative. We cannot design a product, technology, service, or process that everyone will acknowledge as innovative. We can design a product, technology, service, or process that meets the largest number of needs by outperforming its predecessor. By doing such, we will leapfrog competition and establish ourselves as a leader and innovator.

Summary

Defining how individuals perceive innovation as well as using the "means" of innovation was the primary focus of this chapter. Once we understand that perceptions vary for innovation, that variation in understanding can provide a unique competitive advantage. It can also change our lexicon to discuss innovation in terms of what dimensions play a prominent role in our recognition process. Once producers (providers) understand how to transform a product, technology, or service to meet a new or existing need, they can decide to classify which offerings are innovative. Again, for the executive, manager, or project lead, it is not important to try to make everyone recognize that what is offered or sold is innovative. What is important to understand is that the organization should be addressing customer and/or user needs; how the product, service, or technology meets those needs; and how this information can reach the consumer.

Discussion Questions

1. How would you define innovation?
   a. What information do you use to judge a product, technology, or service as innovation?
   b. What experiences do you bring to bear in making an innovation choice or selection?
2. Which theme or dimension would you consider most important for innovation?
3. Consider a product you use nearly every day. What would it take for you to state that the next generation is truly innovative?
4. How well will your organization "transform" itself from the existing paradigm?

Chapter 3

The Innovation Business Ecosystem

Introduction

Most business leaders and managers today understand innovation as a breakthrough product, technology, or service that forever changes the business model and the competitive landscape. Innovation is the product of creative thought. For many innovations, this is true. The problem lies in thinking that innovation is a unique, one-time event. This type of event is unplanned and generally occurs purely by chance (luck). It is only when the stars align, the experts suddenly "create" something unique, or some unexplained event reveals an opportunity that innovation (magically) occurs. Our question at Global Targeting, Inc. is whether you trust "chance" to guide your business and whether the business can afford to trust its existence (or profitability) to luck. If you want more than luck to drive innovation, then consider our perspective and our process for ongoing innovation success.

We see innovation integrated into the business or organization. Rather than existing on the periphery, innovation is at the heart of the business. It is a planned and managed activity encompassing more than the Research and Development (R&D) or Engineering Departments. Innovation should be as frequent in the Human Resources (HR) group as it is in the Engineering Department. Innovation becomes a strategic element of every department.

From our previous chapter, we state clearly that innovation is all about making something better—improving its performance—whether it is a product, process, or person. The word "better" is an evaluation based on the customer's or user's knowledge and experience. If the result also meets a need that is presently unmet, then the user identifies this as innovation. It is not the size or the cost of procuring an innovation that is important; rather, it is the positive result and identified benefit received. The consensus seems to limit innovations to inventions, which may be the reason it is often so infrequent. Within the business and academic community, the meaning of innovation expands beyond inventions to uses and applications.

This expansion of what innovation means places this concept at the heart of the business's or organization's core strategies. Rather than existing as an infrequent event with limited predictability, innovation becomes a driver (a strategy) in the organization. Organizational drivers provide the resources, cash, and personnel for the business to grow and profit. In fact, we see innovation as part of the business "ecosystem." An ecosystem is a self-sustaining environment. The Earth is an ecosystem; it is not self-contained since we need the light from the Sun to exist. Businesses and organizations need cash, customers, and resources to exist and are their own ecosystems (see Figure 3.1).

Innovation is at the heart of the ecosystem. Innovations flow from and to the customer as well as to and from people. This is because innovations come from people (employees) and customers. Those innovations become tangible in either process, product (technology), or service.

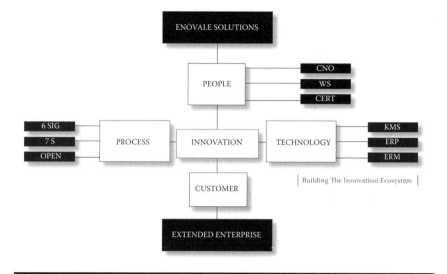

Figure 3.1   Innovation business ecosystem.

Often these innovations exhibit themselves in strategies, techniques, or tools. For products (technologies), numerous innovations come from the applications: KMS (knowledge management systems), ERP (enterprise resource planning) software, or CRM (customer relationship management) software. From the process, there is 6 Sig (Six Sigma and Lean), 7 S (problem-solving methodology), and open (open process) software and applications. Finally, for people, there are those involved with innovation, including the CNO (chief innovation officer), WS (those trained in workshops), and the CERT (certified innovation specialists). Although innovation may use these tools and training, innovation begins and ends with the individual.

The successful organization will build an infrastructure to infuse innovation into the organization at the strategic level. Rather than waiting for a dramatic invention, the organization can move forward with innovations in product (technology), process, or people. Just as functions such as HR, accounting (budgeting), quality, and finance permeate the organization, innovation does as well. Rather than being consigned to

Engineering or Research and Development Departments, innovation becomes a common and expected function. Projects will arise in Engineering as easily as they do in HR. The organizational infrastructure includes innovation as a core competency for all functions and rewards the individual efforts of those employees who actively participate. The creativity unleashed in the business will benefit the organization and provide a distinct competitive advantage, as well as motivate employees to new levels of performance excellence and satisfy them. We expect that some of the profound innovations will come from employees previously prevented from participating in the process. Often, employees best relate to the customer or user.

A successful innovation may not always be a "game changer" for the organization, but it may change the very nature of how the organization operates. This is why we stress numerous performance measures, and we recommend not restricting innovation only to financial performance or market acceptance. When an organization highlights the importance of the individual, dramatic changes in communication, motivation, and performance can lead to increased efficiencies and effectiveness. Incorporating individuals into the innovation process will result in quicker implementations, better alignment, and employees dedicated to innovative practices. Consider an example, in your life, when people came together to solve a problem innovatively. For instance, an emergency results in people performing outside their own expectations. The reason for this performance is the need for action, a focused outcome, and a singularity of purpose. Can you imagine the outcome if the same energy were to be directed toward innovation efforts?

Customers (users) provide both a unique perspective and a contribution from an innovation ecosystem perspective. Customers drive internal innovation (that which occurs in organizations) as well as external innovation, which influences other businesses and the worldwide community. The needs of the customer (user) most often drive internal innovation. The organization or business strives to improve the customer or user experience by providing for his or her needs. At times, though, externally driven innovation may come from a supplier, governmental organization, or entity that also drives innovation. Here, the needs may not necessarily help the customer or user but are generally devised to meet a need that extends beyond the customer to the general population. The need to innovate is one key driver of the organization. One such organization is Choucair Testing (Medellin, Colombia).

At first glance, our client was an excellent test case for our innovation management process. Choucair is a company that has developed external and internal processes that have received many awards for innovation. If what we were touting was legitimate, then this company could try a very different approach to innovation. Our intent was to provide training, help initiate an innovation project, and receive some much needed feedback. We emphasized how individuals understand innovation and how this information would help align teams to achieve innovation success. Fascinated by our "new" approach, Choucair needed proof of concept. They knew innovation was a key business strategy but were not sure how our approach was different from their previous attempts. They had been very successful, and they needed proof that a different approach might be more productive.

One reason we believe that innovation is so infrequent is that no connection exists between the intent to innovate, the customer or user, and product or process. Without these connections, the only outlet is something radically new (such as an invention). We believe that this was the approach taken by Choucair prior to our arrival. Choucair needed innovation but questioned what to do and how to do it. Innovation comes from more than just designated creative people; it can arise from anywhere in the organization.

Another concern, from our experience, is that organizations tend to invent the product, process, or service before it is required (or, worse, needed). Organizations expend resources searching for a use or application, which often leads to an ineffective use of capital. As you will read further, you will fully understand why the need drives the innovation.

The innovation ecosystem diagram (Figure 3.1) also visualizes that product (technology), process, and people are all connected. There is no INnovation without INdividuals and often that innovation will involve both process and product. Figure 3.1 demonstrates the interconnectedness and cohesiveness of these components. This is the primary reason why we say that innovation is more functional in nature than special event oriented. Think of companies such as 3M that constantly innovate. It is part of the corporate culture, allowing their employees time to invent, improve, or change. Others have tried to copy 3M's business model and failed since their leadership considered innovation more project oriented than employee oriented. Changing the existing paradigm is difficult and it will take time. As with any change, the benefits must be obvious. We suggest a trial project, carefully evaluating each step for its benefits and new learning.

The final remaining element in Figure 3.1 is "ENOVALE," the acronym for Global Targeting, Inc.'s proprietary innovation management process. This will be the focus of discussion in Chapter 3 and going forward. We will demonstrate that the ENOVALE® Solutions process enables businesses and organizations to integrate innovation into the organization.

As you read this book, you will better understand how and why we know that innovation is not a unique event, but rather one that can occur naturally and frequently. Most leaders and managers see innovation as a leap forward in their business, whether it is with a new product, technology, or service. The key is to move innovation from a rare event to a managed and planned activity. Innovation becomes strategic functioning and an expected outcome. Employees come to understand the purpose, value, and place that innovation occupies in the organization.

How does one place innovation in this new role? Innovation should be a required goal for all departments (functions) in the organization. Do not try to place a cost or profit estimate on the innovation, at first—such as every department must reduce costs by X% (a typical objective). Benefits of innovation are not equal across the organization. For example, if a project improves employee participation and attitude, there may be no obvious cost savings (only cost expenditure), but the lasting benefit is improved efficiencies and effectiveness. Yes, stress tangible benefits, but do not always assign a cost or profit figure to all innovation.

Six Sigma and Lean suffered from this restrictive objective, resulting in fewer organizations striving for this most worthy goal. The primary emphasis was on cost savings rather than overall benefit. Everyone wants to register a "home run" with every innovation project, but this misses the true incremental learning associated with each project. Maybe a particular department improves communications, alleviating wasted time, inefficiencies, and anxiety. How would one quantify this completely? Therefore, require that innovation generate benefit in whatever form works best for the division, department, or group.

So, what is the key to successful innovation? Is it more allocated funds, more opportunities for good ideas to permeate the organization, or better leadership and management practices? Although all these strategies are helpful, there is clearly no one answer to this baffling question. Consider the following example: While consulting with a large chemical firm and as a part of a Design for Six Sigma improvement project, the team searched for viable application to their existing product. Their product had a single use: a film product placed between two thin layers of glass that becomes automotive safety glass when joined together. Manufactured for many years, the product had been extensively tested and performed well.

Since the project objective required a new product, the team was baffled. Rather than inventing something unique or new, a new use for the existing product was proposed. Redefining innovation permitted the team to discover a new use for an existing product (safety window glass, which is presently used in tens of thousands of homes and businesses). Difficulty arose when the team posed the idea as an innovation and management understood it as an untested and unproven product application. Management nearly killed the project because it perceived that the idea was not innovative, yet it radically changed the business model and refreshed the product life cycle. Can a new use for an existing product be an innovation? In this case, the answer was a resounding YES!

What sustains innovation in an organization is clarifying its meaning and disseminating this knowledge within the organization. Examining innovation through this new lens helps to define its intent and purpose. Leadership needs to remove innovation from its special event status to one that integrates the concept into the organizational mainstream. The best method to explain how innovation exists in an organization is with taxonomy, which is a classification mechanism in the form of a hierarchy. The lower levels are more basic and less descriptive. Innovation from a Global Targeting, Inc. perspective exists in different forms in organizations. The simplest existence for innovation in an organization is when it occurs purely by chance. There is no planning or strategizing, although innovation could be highly prized and even encouraged. The two tiers of innovation (extracted from McLaughlin 2012) are as follows.

Tier 1

- **Loosely defined** (innovation that is loosely tagged or nonexistent)
- **Special event** (innovation due to a specific need or by random occurrence)
- **Departmentalized** (e.g., research and development assigned to a particular department)

Characteristics of tier 1 include the following:

Innovation is seen as an event.

It is discussed and promoted but has no strategic role.

There is inconsistent understanding of the definition and meaning of innovation.

Responsibility is held only at the department level.

Innovation is confused with design and development issues and associated only with products or technology.

Many organizations and businesses remain within the tier 1 framework. We consider this identical to what we experienced in elementary school. Each year a student or team of students would have to create a science-related project. Projects were judged (evaluated) for creativity, accuracy, and content. Those projects judged with a high score would go on to regional science fairs for judgment and a possible reward (prize). In essence, innovation is a "one-time" occurrence—a special event associated only with science. What about other subjects and creativity (yes, we realize that art or music classes exist, but there you need talent)? Other subjects benefit from creativity and innovation. Innovation is just as important in teaching (learning) history as it is for science. Think about a topic in elementary school that you disliked. What were the reasons? Maybe you did not like the teacher or felt the subject was too difficult, or maybe you needed a different approach to learn the subject—now, that is innovation! Many of us operate at tier 1. We think that creativity will come, by chance, to solve a problem. Innovation does not operate best on a "chance" basis but rather through planning and deployment.

Tier 2 is what we believe that businesses and organizations must strive to achieve in today's competitive world. Tier 2 organizations integrate innovation rather than segregating it to only a few departments. These are businesses that constantly innovate—not simply the products (technology) or service offered. Innovation is apparent throughout the organization; embracing it as an effective strategy is just as important as budgetary control and customer responsiveness.

Tier 2

- **Functional** (functions like accounting, finance, and marketing)
- **Strategic** (chief innovation officer plans and projects)
- **Integrated** (full integration into the organizational culture and value system)

Characteristics of tier 2 include the following:

It is strategic; that is, it is planned and funded.
It operates throughout the organization, beginning at the individual level, and is fully integrated with functions similar to HR, finance, etc. (corporate-wide responsibility).
It is real-time, with measured and managed metrics.

Those organizations in tier 2 understand the importance of innovation by integrating it into their functional areas. Tier 2 organizations will be the most successful. Tier 1 organizations (which tend to be the majority) still celebrate innovation as a special event and compartmentalize it to a department or group such as Research and Development. In a world where innovation is a key for success, tier 1 organizations risk much. Remaining ahead of the competition is a strategy proven successful over time. Movement to tier 2 is critical for some industries that must innovate or diminish. Consider which tier best describes your organization at present. If you are in tier 1 but need to be a tier 2 company, what actions will you take to meet this immediate need?

This book will provide a framework for you and your organization to develop a strategy to implement tier 2. It will also describe a process that, when institutionalized, prepares any group, function, or division to innovate on a common and comparable basis. One comment we hear from many CEOs is that innovation efforts are either slow or at a standstill. One executive commented, "We meet and just look at one another as no one knows what steps to take next." We understand their commitment, which is noteworthy, but we also understand why the concept baffles the group. For those individuals, you have the answer in your hands. The answer is not always simple, but it is clear and straightforward. Commitment is required for innovation that requires an understanding that innovation flows to and from the individual. Hiring an innovation leader (which is a good idea from a strategic point) may help coordinate activities, but it does not guarantee success.

Summary

The purpose of this chapter was to introduce the concept of the innovation business ecosystem. Innovation is more than a project; it is truly a strategic initiative. If treated like a project, it will provide some benefit, but eventually this benefit will fade as there is no infrastructure to ensure its success. We use the term "wither" because of its organic nature. As people, process, products, and customers are natural to a company's success, so should innovation be. If introduced as a "program," it will falter over time since it will not receive the full attention of management.

We know that innovation is a topic discussed at all levels and across many businesses. It is a conversation heard in boardrooms and at professional conferences. The talk is voluminous, but the solutions seem rare. We are proposing a proven solution that will work with any organization. Innovation begins and ends with the individual. See for yourself if the strategy seems reasonable and logical. This is all we can ask of you.

Discussion Questions

1. How would your company or organization react to a strategic change in its approach to innovation?
2. Do you believe that your organization can place innovation at the center of its operations?
   a. What barriers do you expect to prevent this from happening?
   b. What will it take to change the "corporate mind-set?"
   c. Which functional group could best lead innovation?
3. What would it take to make an organization move from tier 1 to tier 2?
   a. How drastic would the change be?
      i. Who would support and who would resist?
   b. What is a realistic time frame for implementation?
4. What experiences and knowledge do you use to evaluate innovation?
   a. Does performance enter into your evaluation?
   b. What is the importance you place on meeting new needs (or enhancing existing needs)?

Chapter 4

ENOVALE® Solutions

Introduction

ENOVALE Solutions is a seven-step process for achieving innovation project success (see Figure 4.1). *ENOVALE* is an acronym to help remember the steps in the process; each letter in ENOVALE is the first letter of the first word describing each step. For example, the initial *E* represents step 1: *envision the need*. Each step receives its own description and chapter in this book. Of course, only in English would this acronym be appropriate and correct. Translation into different languages could change the acronym. What is important is that it signifies specific, detailed steps needed for innovation success.

What is the history behind this process? It is actually quite simple: We created the steps and searched for words to describe each step. We wanted a word that no one had ever registered and that did not exist in the dictionary—something people could remember and associate with innovation. That is it—nothing more complicated.

The process of creating the steps was much lengthier. Unlike a well known technique such as Six Sigma, which begins with a problem and ends with an improvement, innovation projects begin with fulfilling a need or set of needs.

Figure 4.1 ENOVALE innovation process management steps.

The purpose is not to "fix" or solve a problem. Yet, techniques such as Six Sigma rely on evidence and validation to make changes to a process. Using past history as a tool, we examined both successful and unsuccessful innovation projects. What made one project a "winner" and another a "loser?" We knew that management support, a clear set of objectives and requirements, and a team that could easily align to a project outcome were critical. In addition, measurement, validation, and strong ties to organizational performance goals were a necessity. Keep these issues in mind as you read through the book, as you will see the logic and common sense we applied.

To bring ENOVALE into the workplace it had to be a simple but effective process. Management is searching for that process that can ensure more innovative projects with greater benefits. The process is not just a set of steps or phases but it also challenges predisposed ideas regarding innovation. No one department can generate all the innovation projects. A project must come from the individual but also meet criteria for it to become a worthy project. This challenges the status quo, brings more people into the innovation circle, and applies a much less opinionated approach for project acceptance. What is most fulfilling is how executives and managers identify with the process and support its tenets. We were amazed by how it changes the perspective of others, allowing them to understand that this is a strategy applicable across the organization. For one of our clients, it brought an entirely new perspective on innovation. This is what we believe will be the success of ENOVALE.

In a more practical sense, the ENOVALE Solutions process has two major functions. First, it provides a transformative road map for organizations to develop and produce innovative outcomes. It has successfully changed management's understanding of the concept of innovation and the steps needed to achieve innovative outcomes. The process has changed people (management) to view innovation from a functional and strategic perspective.

The second purpose is far more utilitarian: It provides an ongoing process for creating and evaluating innovative projects. Of course, we are asked, "Why so many steps?" and we constantly remind our clients that this method applies solely to innovation projects. A frequent question is, "Can we apply this to all projects?" We say yes, but warn that the time required is more than for a standard project. We want to keep innovation projects separate and unique from standard projects. The process also provides a set of tools that can serve other purposes in the organization. One client told us that it used these tools to decide which projects (non-innovation) to fund in the next fiscal year.

ENOVALE will signify a commitment to successful and sustained innovation. Leaders, managers, and those responsible for implementing innovation across the organization already use the ENOVALE Solutions process. It is a blueprint for success. Team leaders, team members, and even individuals are conducting successful innovation projects using ENOVALE Strategies. Chapter 12 provides an abbreviated description of this strategy.

Once the project need is established, it is time to agree on a unified definition of innovation. For example, say that there is a need to improve the billing process. We know from the statement of the need that we will follow a strategy that improves the process. Each theme of innovation requires its own unique strategy. In fact, those who use the same strategy for all types of innovation will eventually fail. The strategy for the next version of the iPad is much different from a changeover of key personnel. Be aware of the type of innovation driving the need.

One of the key discoveries that we made in our research and development of the ENOVALE methodologies is that service businesses find it a challenge to apply innovation in a services environment. The problem stems from the definition of innovation as an invention that drives organizations dominated by technology or manufacturing. These organizations produce tangible products, using many of the five senses. The tangible nature of the product produces simpler performance measures and therefore is often easier to judge. From an innovation standpoint, individuals can better judge if their needs are met with tangible items. That is, producers begin with raw materials; create a process to refine, integrate, or manufacture parts; and deliver finished goods to their customers. These products have features and functions easily translated into benefits for the user; they have distinctive, tangible attributes that establish specifications related to performance. This provides opportunities for feedback and review. Customers buy these products based on something that fulfills a need or that they find appealing. It is simpler to evaluate performance and apply innovative improvements or changes to the development or manufacturing process.

Service companies are different. The services they deliver are intangible, often lacking tangible measures of performance. Certainly, measures such as time, numbers in a queue, number of service agents, etc. are tangible, but they are incomplete when evaluating the service. Individuals use knowledge from past encounters and present experiences to judge whether the service was effective. Intangibility is more difficult to define and measure, yet customers and users know when they are satisfied. Judging whether a service is effective (satisfying) requires that a customer's encounter exceed what the customer expected.

Evaluating service innovation requires a more discriminating judgment. For a service to be innovative, it must not only meet a new need (or fulfill an existing need) but also far exceed the expectations of the individual familiar with the previous service (or similar encounter). The difficulty is in measuring (judging) how "far" that expectation must exceed previous encounters or experiences. Knowing the customer will provide insight into how this value is measured.

When looking at any organization within the corporate innovation ecosystem (see Figure 4.1), one still has to apply the people, process, technology, and customer perspective. Thus, customers are still the ultimate judges in deeming the innovative value of a service. People provide validation of the value that ENOVALE brings to the innovation process for a services company, because innovation initiatives align the right people to achieve predictable and measurable innovation outcomes.

In ENOVALE terms, it is about the individual. Innovation in service businesses refers to people or process or both. The individual will judge a service innovative if it meets a need and delivers performance better than expected. Therefore, the service provider must understand what the service provides (its tangible elements) and its intangible elements (the difference between what we expect versus what we encounter).

Applying ENOVALE to the services industry became an important undertaking for Global Targeting, Inc. One such service business is the outsourcing industry, which is a perfect fit for ENOVALE because the industry has gone from delivering cost-effective solutions to having to provide more value now. Innovative efforts can increase value and provide those in the industry with more than they expect.

Summary

Understanding innovation from the perspective of this chapter changes the approach to ensuring a successful project. Innovation from a three-element (dimension) approach permits a corporate- or organization-wide implementation strategy. No longer consigned to the next invention, now innovation can occur throughout the organization, from large companies to small. In addition, all departments can participate, rather than only those associated with research or engineering.

Innovation generates transformation in people, process, technology, and service. This is the key difference between improvement strategies such as Six Sigma and Lean, which work within the process to improve performance. Transforming a product or service is the responsibility of the organization (whether business, nonprofit, or governmental entity) to meet new or existing needs. Individuals recognize innovation in the products, technology, and service they purchase and use. Figure 4.2 defines the transformative role of ENOVALE.

Given that individuals initiate innovation based on a need, training and supporting individuals to develop their creative talents becomes a corporate goal. This talent pool becomes a competitive advantage as innovations become routine. Employees interested in extending themselves can support the organization's growth and profitability. Rather than waiting for the next innovation, the organization is generating success after success.

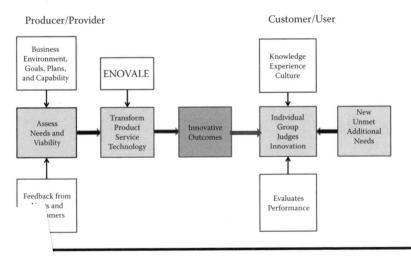

Innovation outcome model.

Discussion Questions

1. How would you define innovation and how would your definition differ from that which most people associate with innovation?
2. How difficult will it be for you to distinguish an innovation project?
   a. What are the strengths of a successful project?
   b. What are its weaknesses?
3. What convincing argument can you make for ENOVALE?
4. Is your organization ready for the transformative ENOVALE process?

Chapter 5

"E" Envision the Need

Introduction

The first step in the ENOVALE® Solutions process is to Envision the need. We could easily use the letter "E" to mean "establish the need," as this has the same meaning. Innovation begins with a need; the need drives the innovation. Specific needs come from the internal organization and the external customer. Needs are the catalysts and initiating factors for innovation. These needs can be as simple as the need for shelter or as complex as the need for massive computational storage in a small container. All innovations came from some need. Even the most basic, fire, was an innovation for those living at that time. Using fire for cooking and warmth was truly more of a discovery. The innovation was the method to initiate the fire and keep it burning. The need was for fire and for the methods needed to contain and control the fire for future use. Consider the power to control fire for cooking, preserving, heating, defense, barter, etc. The ability to initiate and control the fire gave the person or group a powerful advantage. Because it met so many crucial needs, it also became the envy of surrounding peoples. The need to initiate and maintain the fire drove the innovation; fire already existed! This is the first element of the ENOVALE Solutions process: First, identify the need(s).

For those of us lucky enough to be living in the twenty-first century, our needs have become very sophisticated, and this now drives innovation. We search for those innovations that simplify or make our lives easier and better (safer, richer, more fulfilling, increased leisure time, etc.). Innovations drive society and its achievements. The question, though, is how to use innovation to meet more of our present and future needs. How can we ensure that innovation becomes routine (part of our lives that enriches our well-being) rather than just a special event? For most organizations, innovation is a special event, one that is uncommon and often unplanned. For innovation to become routine within the organization, there need to be a commitment and a plan (strategy) for accomplishing this objective.

Although ENOVALE Solutions is a seven-step strategic plan, commitment and support from leadership are essential. Our experience with business leaders is that commitment is forthcoming if an available and workable plan exists. The description of this process and its requirements provides leadership with the tools and resources to make innovation a routine function that can be planned and monitored and is responsive to the needs of the organization.

Envisioning the Need

To envision the need requires a comprehensive understanding of the term innovation (described in Chapter 2). Whatever the innovation, it must begin by fulfilling a particular need. Specific needs emanate from individuals. The ability to light a darkened room without the use of fire (a candle or gas lamp) was unthinkable for most of the nineteenth century. Edison achieved the unattainable by creating the first "working" light bulb. The need drove this invention and the improvements (innovations) that have occurred since his time. Edison's light bulb also needed an energy source (electricity), which was a major innovation (derived from a need to have a constant energy source). The need provides the purpose and reason for the innovation.

Consider how the need drove the innovation that produced the wheel. The need was for transportation involving both people and goods. Many inventors or innovators considered the need and probably devised many unique adaptations of rocks, wood, or other materials. It was easy to understand that a round shape could travel easily—but how to use the wheel to transport goods and people? Bing (n.d.) defines the wheel as "rotating round part: a ring or disk that revolves or is turned by a central shaft or pin, sometimes with a central hub that has radiating spokes attached to a circular rim." The true invention was the wheel and shaft (pin). Obviously, we do not know who invented the wheel; we only know when it appeared. The need created the initiative to innovate a reusable wheel for transportation. When considering the need, think about what existed for transportation: animals, brute strength, rivers, and streams—all of which were limiting in some regard. Interestingly, the wealthy did not need this simple innovation as much as the masses. However, even their lives improved as transportation improved and radically changed all facets of society.

Human needs have always driven progress and technology throughout the ages. In fact, human needs have far outweighed our available resources and technology. Society evolved to control and/or allocate resources for a purpose (although not always the most noble). We call the available resources "supply," while our needs are "demands." Human needs create demand and demand (which is tangible) drives our economy. It is the interaction of needs (demand) and resources (supply) that creates innovation. The previous statement is not a definition that you would find in a standard dictionary! When a need exists and is plausible, available resources become possible. Of course, the need must be within the reach of available technology. Star Trek's transporter is a better option than a car, airplane, or boat, but the technology to create it is not yet available.

Human needs drive the purpose for innovation. To increase their mobility, humans had to innovate. People could have improved the animals they were using (faster, carrying heavier loads), or they could have moved themselves nearer to a river for transportation. Finally, they could have invented something that solved their needs: The wheel remains a viable component of transportation.

The study of needs has received a great deal of attention. Maslow developed a famous hierarchy (in order of importance) of needs in 1943 because he wanted to provide an explanation of basic needs (see Figure 5.1).

The most basic of needs are food, shelter, and clothing, listed as physiological needs. The next level is safety needs (protection, safety, etc.) and then the need for companionship (love of family, community, etc.), and finally the personal needs of self-esteem and self-actualization. Needs drive innovations, so innovations can occur at any level of Maslow's

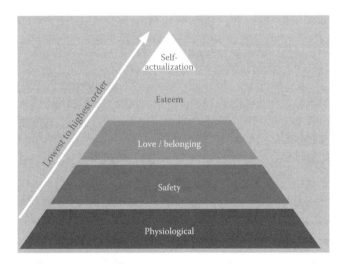

Figure 5.1 Maslow's hierarchy of needs. (Adapted from Golanz, S., and C. R. Bowen. 2011. *Industrial Engineer* Oct.: 45–48.)

hierarchy. The majority are at the basic levels associated with physiological and safety needs. These needs have driven civilizations to find the resources to meet the needs. The drive to meet these needs has resulted in great discoveries as well as great wars and savage behavior. Needs have driven society to invent, improve, and change lifestyles and behaviors. Needs provide the rationale or reasoning for the innovation. Start the process by envisioning the need.

Needs are driven at the organizational level as well. These needs can be external in nature (from the customer or user) or internal (the organization). Innovation can come from either of these two sources. In either case, needs must benefit an end user. External needs drive most projects, as this is how the company gains competitive advantage and improves its profit. However, internally, a project may benefit the user and the organization. A focus on organizational proficiency, employee advancement, and efficiencies of scale may greatly benefit the organization, but have little effect on the bottom line. Management willing to accept the benefits in lieu of those that expand the business exhibit an understanding of innovation not frequently demonstrated or rewarded.

Do Ideas Drive Innovation?

Many people make the mistake of thinking that innovations come purely from creative ideas (and, of course, many do) without first developing the need. An idea is a thought or inspiration. It remains an intangible unless it can exist in the physical realm. Mathematicians, scientists, and researchers create ideas that must explain a phenomenon, define a theory, or identify a concept. These inventions still provide meaning and explanation for our existing in a physical world. Now, pair the idea with a need and you have all the components to initiate the innovation! The innovation takes the intangible (the idea) and links it directly with the tangible (a need) to bring into the physical world. Just creating ideas, on their own, is a valuable exercise but it remains an intangible until it embraces a human need.

An idea may be a great place to begin, but what if my idea was a wearable blanket? We know this is a successful idea, but the need to keep warm long preceded this idea. Ideas without specific needs are not always marketable (yes, they may make for great examples or stories); ideas are not innovation. Many believe that innovation begins with ideas and structured programs to capture these ideas. Many of the best ideas or suggestions go untested because the obvious need was unknown or ill considered. Once the need is established, then solicit ideas and suggestions—this is the time for creativity. There are numerous and published incidences of corporate programs to elicit ideas (suggestions). These ideas should provide the framework for innovation, yet over time they become less and less effective (for one organization, idea generation produced 40% of the innovations in the first year and only 10% in the third; Dahl, Lawrence, and Pierce 2011).

Generating ideas is useful (and part of the ENOVALE process)—but not before first identifying the need. Needs are generated by wants or desires. By establishing the need, you will clearly differentiate yourself from competitors accustomed to a successful idea generating an invention. In addition, this will help to devise that revolutionary solution that will provide a definitive product, service, process, or decision with significant cost advantages. Innovations derived from needs are more successful because they have a specific purpose and reason for existence.

Use the following set of questions as a method to identify critical needs that require an innovative approach.

1. Is the customer requesting a specific new product or technology, or an improvement to an existing process (examples of processes include billing, communications, project management, delineation of specifications, etc.)?

2. Is there a new product or technology, improved process, or change that would provide a competitive advantage?
3. Do existing organizational strategies support future growth? Would a change provide beneficial returns?
4. What external needs does the organization require for continuing profitability, growth, cost containment, technical superiority, etc.?
5. What external needs require immediate improvement or change?
6. Is performance an issue with internal processes?
   a. When performance falls below expectations, how does the organization react?
7. Would changes in management style or behavior benefit the organization?

After defining the need, consider the purpose it will serve. This will help refine the type of innovation required: It will define the innovation. For those in the product or service sectors, the customer or the user generally generates this information. Remember that customers (users) cannot define the innovation (the technology, new product, or service), but only the specific need. This is why we warn organizations to reconsider projects and activities that have no defined customer or user need. If there is no identified need, there is no reason to apply the ENOVALE Solutions process.

Unfulfilled Needs

No one or no organization can fill all needs. Innovation begins with a fulfilled need. Innovations can also flow from a set of unfulfilled needs. An unfulfilled need is a need that is unmet or incomplete. It remains a need until the resources or technologies (or both) are available to fulfill the need. Since needs arise from individuals, individuals are the best resource to identify these needs.

From an innovation standpoint, an unfulfilled need is an opportunity. Consider the following simple example: There is a need for cars that can drive themselves. This would vastly reduce highway deaths, injuries, insurance costs, traffic congestion, commute time, etc. It would assist those disabled persons incapable of driving a car at present. There are many positives. Even jet aircraft today are so sophisticated that they can taxi, take off, fly, and land without pilot assistance. Therefore, the idea of cars driving themselves is not impossible, only an unfulfilled need.

Ask yourself the following questions regarding unfulfilled needs:

1. What does the customer need that is not being provided at this time?
2. What is preventing the organization from acting on these needs?
   a. Capacity or capability issues?
   b. Unavailable resources?
   c. Outside the organization's purpose and mission?
   d. Outside the technical bounds of the organization?
3. What fulfilled need would increase business and provide lasting opportunity?
4. What are the needs that customers do not realize they truly want?

Unfulfilled needs are essentially an innovation wish list. Many will never see "the light of day," but a few may hold true value. Regularly ask your users or customers what they need that is presently unavailable. Ask them for their wish lists with regard to the product or service you provide. Do the same with your employees or colleagues. First, think within your industry and about your customer; second, think about the needs that your organization would like to fulfill ("think outside the box"); third, think about what your organization cannot fulfill; and, finally, identify the opportunities that arise from this information. Filter the list with criteria built with organizational expertise, knowledge, and common sense. Keep these suggestions secure.

Discussion Questions

Use these questions to understand your or your organization's priorities as they apply to needs and plan to address these needs. Prior to beginning the ENOVALE process, consider your business or organizational (and personal) goals and objectives.

1. How do your business or organizational plans (strategies) address specific needs?
2. Is there a direct link between needs driven externally or internally?
3. Which unfulfilled needs require new technology, processes, or people?
4. Which needs are possible and impossible to meet at this time?
5. How do needs integrate well with organizational values?

Upon defining and elaborating a need, use the information to categorize the innovation into one of three themes discussed previously. The first described is that associated with "new" innovations or inventions.

"New" Innovations

Inventions and/or a novel idea are unique—one of a kind. New products or services fulfill a new need or a need that was unfulfilled. We consider that innovations can occur in three distinct new ways: Something very new, a new application or concept, or a new approach. Each of these depends on the amount of originality—something that is completely original and has never existed. Originality can also exist with new uses and new approaches. For original concepts:

1. The need must be unique; there are no substitutes available.
2. The innovation will require a new or different way of thinking.
3. The innovation comes from the mind of the inventor or designer through an idea or concept.
4. The need drives the creative forces—the strongest for this type of innovation.

Formalize the need; be as specific as possible. Needs must be viable, capable and sustainable. Refine the needs by applying a set of evaluative criteria.

Viability: Criteria that assesses feasibility and practicality issues
Capability: Criteria that assesses performance issues
Sustainability: Criteria that assesses the length of time the innovation is competitive

Use multiple criteria to judge potential success and failure. It is critical to rely on measurable criteria rather than opinion or conjecture. Innovation is something that begins at the human level but requires evaluation with a set of measurable criteria. Table 5.1 lists criteria to assess and then refine the need.

Consider an Example: Suppose a need existed for a totally hands-free cell phone, with the electronics located within a piece of clothing (set as a belt). Select each major criterion and determine if the need has the potential to be a reality.

Opinions are gut feelings and can be valuable decision tools but not for something as dynamic as innovation. Fully evaluate needs, objectives, and requirements or face the possibility of failure. Consider an example: GPS (global positioning system) tracks objects very differently from radar or by radio waves. The technology filled a specific need to replace or augment

Table 5.1   Needs Assessment for "New" Innovation

Need's Assessment Criteria for New Products or Processes/ New Technology/New Services	
Viability	**Assessment/Acceptance**
Distinctiveness	
Creativeness	
Producible	
Reproducible by competitors	
Capability	
Competitiveness	
Profitability/cost effectiveness	
ROI	
Recurring Income	
Outperform existing items	
High reliability	
Sustainability	
Long-life cycle	
Safety	
Environmental/Legal protection	
Complexity	
Time before replacement/replacement	
Other criteria	

a system that was not always precise or without problems. The GPS was new, and its application required new technology.

Inventing something new is not simple; it requires experience, expertise, and creative thinking. Over time, one can easily develop these skills. Using criteria provides a mechanism to evaluate innovation. Obviously, each innovation will have its own specific set of criteria to evaluate its potential.

Decision-makers must rely on criteria rather than emotion to increase their chances for success. Specific and detailed criteria add a filtering mechanism, providing an initial set of requirements related to overall "fitness for use."

"Improved Innovations"

Improvements—whether in process, product, or service—have been an item of discussion since the early parts of the last century. Fredrick Taylor, as a means to improve both productivity and efficiency, introduced the "scientific method." Since that time, legendary authors such Shewhart, Deming, Crosby, Juran, and others have devised methods to improve processes and resultant performance. Improvements such as Six Sigma and Lean methods continue the rich legacy of these tools and philosophies. Although this type of improvement continues to be critical, the discussion for this section focuses on innovative improvements.

Innovative improvements are those improvements that specifically increase performance. The process sustains greater efficiencies, produces more, costs less or it improves overall effectiveness. The need drives the improvement since it is performing below expectations (but within acceptable performance limits). The distinguishing characteristic of innovative improvement is that the process, product, or service needs to perform better. The ENOVALE® techniques work best for improvements when the need requires better than expected performance. A new performance level will result in either competitive advantage or significant cost savings. Unlike techniques such as Six Sigma and Lean which identify problems (inefficiencies) causing performance issues, innovative improvements increases performance beyond accepted norms. Customers and users will recognize the improved performance as innovative. Improvements, using the ENOVALE® process are more adaptive and collaborative.

As with the ENOVALE® Solutions process, we begin with the need for something to exceed existing performance. Much like with the previous section, apply the three criteria to refine the need (See Table 5.2). Each project brings its own elements of viability, capability, and sustainability. Customers and end users can often assist in defining or

Table 5.2   Needs Assessment for "Improved" Innovation

Need's Assessment Criteria for Improved Products or Processes/ New Technology/New Services	
Viability	**Assessment/Acceptance**
Performance exceeds that of competitors	
Process requires minimal adaptation	
Solvable problem	
Implementable Solution	
Profitability	
ROI	
Capability	
Robustness	
Minimal implementation Time	
Minimal Costs (All types)	
Available Resources	
Performance exceeds that of competitors	
Sustainability	
Long life-cycle	
Performance not easy to replicate	
Root cause solution	
Competitive and technical Awareness	
Other criteria	

refining these specific elements. For improvement, define the three criteria as:

Viability: Criteria that assesses feasibility and practicality issues

Capability: Criteria that assesses performance issues (over or under performance)

Sustainability: Criteria that assesses the length of time the innovation is competitive

It is critical to get in the habit of associating needs with criteria that evaluate its effectiveness, benefit, and longevity. This provides for a mechanism for refinement, clarification, and selection. If needs exist but are outside the capacity and capability of the organization, then a project has little chance of success. If, however, the needs meets these criteria then the project greatly increases its chances for success. By evaluating needs, the organization greatly reduces false starts and mis-steps at this early stage of the ENOVALE process.

What is an improved innovation? A cell phone is an excellent example of innovative improvement over time. Cell phones continue to act as small radios with both a transmitter and receiver. Consider the improvements in 20 years streaming video, instant e-mail, games, TV, GPS. This is not to say that there is no new technology applied but the cell phone is constantly improving with services and offerings. These constant improvements are enhancements; however, the basic principle remains the same. When considering needs that meet the improvement criteria, consider first existing performance and then decide upon the item that needs improvement.

"Change Innovation"

Innovative change replaces what exists with a positive outcome. There are many definitions of "change" (the verb to: alter, modify, amend, exchange, etc.). Innovative change takes on the meaning to swap, replace, substitute, or switch what has existed with something different. Innovative change always results in a positive outcome.

Innovative change replaces what exists (a process, a product/service, a person) with a comparable process, product/service, or person. One key element of innovative change is the decision involved in choosing the item or person to replace and the solution implemented. Therefore, the decision becomes a major element of the innovation process. The proposed change initiates a decision and that decision affects the outcome. Therefore, innovative change is positive when the outcome is positive. A positive outcome can be improved performance (cost, efficiency, delivery) communications, motivation, or satisfaction. There is a pronounced human element to this dimension of innovation.

Outsourcing is a great example of innovative change especially if the outcome is positive. The ENOVALE model begins with a need, selects the right person, creates the outcome based on its requirements, validates the outcome, and aligns the individuals or users linking these to performance. Change is the result of an event that requires decisive action (a decision). Change affects individuals most and, for many, is a negative experience to avoid. What we propose is change recognized as innovative; the result is replacing the existing situation with something better (positive).

We all experience change throughout our lives—some good and some not so well. Positive change is truly innovative as it transforms (replaces) a situation from negative or neutral to a positive outcome. How often has a new boss, supervisor, or leader changed the existing environment by improving communications, motivating employees or increased productivity? When this occurs, people, situations, attitudes, and the overall environment transforms. The result is truly innovative and perceived by those affected by the change. In fact, our research validates that this is most often the most powerful element (or theme) of innovation. The reason it affects individuals is that it is more tangible to them. They "live" the outcome on a daily basis.

As with other elements of Innovation, the need drives the innovation. Traditionally, management initiates the change is a management through initiating a decision. The change occurs, and the organization must adjust to the decision and its consequences. From our experience, the majority of occurrences produce negative or neutral results, at best. At times, this is unavoidable. However, there are numerous opportunities for positive outcomes—that is, innovative change.

Therefore, evaluate a needed change with specific criteria. Never initiate a major decision with emotion or opinion. If someone uses the words, "I feel" or "I think" then emotion or opinion will overtake the decision process. There must be tangible reasons for change that will benefit the organization. Therefore, evaluate the proposed change initiatives with the following criteria:

Viability: Criteria that assesses continuance with minimal repercussions (consequences)

Capability: Criteria that assesses performance issues (efficiency, effectiveness)

Sustainability: Criteria that assesses the length of time the innovation is positive

When considering change, be aware of alternative solutions. Alternatives are decisions with different outcomes than the proposed decision. An alternative is not just the "flip side" of the original decision but guarantees a different outcome. Assess any decision and its consequences with a viable alternative, even if the alternative seems impossible. Frequently, a decision to change creates alternatives that are equally acceptable. With every alternative comes a new set of consequences, opportunities, and possible repercussions.

For some, the thought of evaluating a potential decision seems frivolous. Yet, positive change can have such a lasting impact on an organization or an individual (see Table 5.3).

The power of the word "Change" is truly transformative. Changes can be subtle or revolutionary. Change that benefits the organization and the individual is truly innovative. The permanency of change is dramatic, but its nature is to be transitional. It is rarely subtle and more often experienced as drastic. Change directly affects the individual, which is at the center of innovation. Using the ENOVALE Solutions process

Table 5.3 Needs Assessment for Innovative Change

Need's Assessment Criteria for Innovative Change	
Viability	**Assessment/Acceptance**
Ongoing failures	
Economic/business conditions	
Challenges the status-quo	
Effect on customers/users	
Motivation/Productivity	
Availability of Alternatives	
Capability	
Reduced performance	
Lost efficiencies/effectiveness	
Instability	
Sustainability	
Significant Benefit	
Timeliness	
Solves recurring problem(s)	
Other criteria	

to initiate innovative change is transformative providing a "blueprint" or model for future change.

Summary

The first step in the ENOVALE Solutions process is critical for success as it drives innovation from a needs perspective. Figure 5.2 details the main components of this first step. Needs drive the innovation and viability, capability and sustainability provide the mechanism for evaluation. The more the need is refined and developed, through the needs analysis process, the better the chance of making the proper decision. Incorporating the individual, you bring his or her experiences, expertise, and buy-in to the project and its consequences.

Envisioning and then establishing the need provides the reasoning, justification, and logic for developing

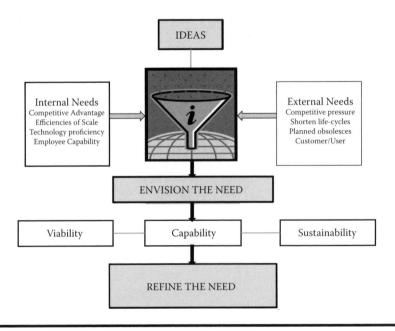

Figure 5.2 The "envision the need" process step.

the innovation. It also established a precedent for future innovative ideas that must meet a set of criteria before moving forward. Ideas are creative, but without a specific need, an idea remains just an idea. The journey of connecting needs with ideas is often the least travelled path. Innovation is more than an idea it is a need that generates ideas for a specific purpose.

After each chapter of the ENOVALE process, we pose a series of discussion questions for our readers. The intent is that our readers will reflect on these questions reviewing the materials and resources in each Chapter. These questions require some thought, and your answers may differ from others in your organization. This demonstrates the power of perceptions and the potential conflict that can arise from two very distinctive interpretations of a similar concept. When you experience this difference, you will best understand why innovation is so individually driven.

Discussion Questions

Use these questions to understand how you or your organizational sets priorities as it applies to needs.

1. What needs does your business or organization require to leapfrog their competition?
2. Is there a direct link between external needs and internal needs?
3. Do these needs require new technologies, new processes, or different people?
4. Consider any unfulfilled needs—what is possible and impossible at this time?
5. Do needs integrate well with organizational values?
6. Ask a small group to individually define Innovation. Compare and contrast the differences in perception and understanding. Look for opportunities to align. What did you learn from this exercise?

7. Identify an innovation that is new, an improvement or a distinctive (positive) change?
   a. What are the distinguishing characteristics?
   b. How could individuals differ in their understanding (or interpretation) of innovation?

Chapter 6

"N" Nominate

Introduction

Phase 2 of the ENOVALE® Solutions process directs innovation to the organic or atomic level. As stated previously, innovation begins with the individual or group of individuals with a similar mind-set. Phase 2 identifies those individuals who have similar perceptions (understanding) of innovation. Envisioning, defining, and then refining the need permits the nomination and selection process to begin. The need will identify the innovation theme or dimension providing a framework from which to nominate group members. A survey of individuals determines their understanding of innovation and support for organizational values. Selecting individuals occurs after analyzing survey results that evaluate understanding of innovation, work environment, and organizational value assessment.

Analysis of the survey assigns individuals to one of three innovation dimensions, depending upon the strength of the individual's scores. Individuals with similar scores are identified as potential team members for the project team. When perceptions align, individuals will have a similar mind-set about a concept such as innovation. Aligned perceptions increase project completion time. After the need has been established and its effectiveness and viability been evaluated, the process of selecting individuals can begin. Selecting the "right" or best aligned individual to the dimension of innovation ensures improvements in efficiency and effectiveness. When like-minded people work in a team with the goal of achieving a specific objective, possibilities are endless.

Consider the fact that, in 1961, President John F. Kennedy requested that, within the decade, NASA not only land a man on the moon, but also return him safely. At that time, the Soviet Union had demonstrated significant technical achievement in space and was gaining a technical edge over the United States. The actual need was for the United States was to demonstrate technical superiority over the Soviet Union. NASA had less than 10 years to meet this objective. President Kennedy gave NASA a specific objective, based on a very critical need; they had to design and build the equipment, test it, and certify it as safe. NASA assembled a team of engineers and scientists (like-minded individuals) with a specific need (or goal, if you prefer). We know they were successful, but what was their secret for success? At least four critical items had to be available:

1. Funding
2. Clear goals and outcomes
3. Aligned perceptions with a sole purpose (a specific need)
4. Supportive management

Because of this effort, thousands of inventions (particularly those related to electronic miniaturization), safety improvements, and changes to how humans cope in an inhospitable environment became available for everyday use. We continue to benefit from the space program and its new technologies. Innovations occurred because the objective or goal (need) was clear, resources were made available, and support from government persisted. This example explains why selecting (nominating) the right persons is so critical for sustained innovation success. Select individuals because they value innovation, can perform within the existing work environment, and want to add value to the project goal. This formula continues to work and can be applied to any organization.

Selecting the Correct Individuals— Understanding of Innovation

For our proprietary clients, we have developed a survey that provides information on how individuals understand and apply innovation and assess work environment attitudes and organizational values. In addition, we provide the company with suggestions for selecting the best individuals for the innovation project. Our client, Choucair Testing, participated in the proprietary survey process. Administering a survey company-wide is a difficult task, given the need for both management and employee buy-in. More than 150 individuals responded and we were able to compare these data for our ongoing global studies to establish a baseline.

Their results were quite similar to our previous findings that stated a difference between generations (generational difference for a South American sample). Interestingly, for a high-tech company accustomed to many innovations, the responses were similar to those found in our global research. We did include a question on where innovation begins in the organization. The answers surprised us, as the respondents clearly said it could start with any group or function. It verified our data statement that innovation begins and ends with individuals. For more explanation, contact Global Targeting, Inc. for a detailed proprietary survey including the analysis used to identify potential team members.

In this book, we provide similar surveys, which any organization can apply. These surveys will provide key information to assist in selecting the individuals best aligned with the innovation project intent. Begin the selection process by asking interested participants to take two short surveys. The purpose of the first survey (Table 6.1) is to identify the type of innovation best

Table 6.1 Innovation Assessment Survey Coding

Statement Number	Instructions: Check the box that best matches your agreement (disagreement) with each statement that defines innovation	Strongly Disagree	Disagree	Neither Disagree nor Agree	Agree	Strongly Agree
1	Something that is an invention					
2	Making something better					
3	Replacing what is not working					
4	Something new, novel, or unique					
5	Constantly improving (making something better)					
6	Changing for the better					
7	Improving something to make it better					
8	Changing what does not work					
9	Something never seen before					

understood. This is how the individual perceives and characterizes innovation from a three-theme (dimensional) perspective. The second assesses perceptions of what individuals value. The surveys provided in this chapter are a shortened version of proprietary Global Targeting surveys used worldwide to assess perceptions of what innovation means to the individual. These surveys will provide useable information on the first step in identifying prospective team members. Have respondents check the response that best matches their perceptions of innovation. When coding the data (Table 6.2), identify each response with a numerical value, using the survey coding valuation.

To determine how the three specific statements describe each innovation element (dimension), follow the instructions given in Table 6.3. The largest average score describes

Table 6.2   Survey Coding Values

Survey Response	Coded Value
Strongly disagree	1
Disagree	2
Neither disagree nor agree	3
Agree	4
Strongly agree	5

Table 6.3   Innovation Dimension Calculation

Innovation Dimension or Theme	Mean (average) of Statements Range of Statements
New	(Statement 1 + Statement 4 + Statement 9) ÷ 3 Range = largest to smallest value
Improve	(Statement 2 + Statement 5 + Statement 7) ÷ 3 Range = largest to smallest value
Change	(Statement 3 + Statement 6 + Statement 8) ÷ 3 Range = largest to smallest value

the individual's strongest understanding of innovation.
The survey, by design, skews scores toward the "strongly agrees"
scale. The scores can be interpreted as follows:

- Average score below 3.0: limited understanding of the
  concept or no support
- Average of 3.0–3.9: marginal understanding of the concept
- Average of 4.0–4.5: understands and supports the
  concept
- Average above 4.5: understands well and greatly supports
  the concept

Score each innovation dimension (theme) separately.
Carefully consider your interpretation (see Table 6.4).
Remember that small samples will not show large average
differences. If the averages are very similar for the three
themes, then examine each statement score separately; evaluate the minimum and maximum values for each dimension.
Composite (theme) scores with less variation (using the
range) indicate consistency. Consider the simple example in
Table 6.4.

Naturally, "change" has the largest average, but it also has
more variability. Notice that "new" has no variation (range is
defined as the largest value to smallest value) with a range = 0.
This would be the best choice due to the consistency of
response by the individual and the fact that the average of
statements for "change" (the largest average score) is not
above 4.5.

Table 6.4   Interpreting Average Scores

Innovation Dimension or Theme	Mean (average) and Range of Statements
New	$(4 + 4 + 4) \div 3 = 4$; range = 0
Improve	$(5 + 4 + 3) \div 3 = 4$; range = 2
Change	$(3 + 5 + 5) \div 3 = 4.33$; range = 2

If the patterns are difficult to interpret, then proceed with a short interview. Ask the candidate a few questions:

1. What does the word innovation mean to you personally?
2. What are the most important and least important definitions of innovation to you? Why?
3. If you did not consider the innovation project important, how difficult would it be to work on this project?

Misalignment of how an individual understands the meaning of innovation will cause problems and project delays, resulting in

■ Lost time
■ Ineffectiveness
■ Reduced productivity
■ Communication issues
■ Human issues (motivation, trust, prioritization, job realignment, etc.)

Selecting individuals based on non-innovation-related criteria could have an adverse effect. Using criteria such as job titles, favoritism, functional roles, opinions, etc. can cause potential problems. You need aligned individuals who understand the purpose and reason for the proposed innovation project and whose values reflect these beliefs. In order to facilitate a decision, we recommend that management distribute a values survey in tandem with the innovation survey. Global Targeting, Inc. has created a values-innovation survey that measures agreement with corporate (organizational) values and innovation project goals.

Selecting the Correct Individuals—Values Assessment

Remember that individuals value what they support and, if they support a culture of innovation, then these persons become viable candidates. It may seem counterintuitive to use a perceptual survey to select individuals, but remember that this device removes emotion and opinion from the initial selection process. It provides empirical data for comparison and selection purposes (see Table 6.5).

Assign a numerical value to each possible response. Use the same coding as with the innovation comprehension survey and the scoring guide (Table 6.2). For this survey, there are two dimensions: organizational values and individual values. The first five statements reflect support for organization value. The remaining five statements assess individual perceptions of value as it relates to project success—that is, the ability to support objectives, priorities, and team goals.

Those with the largest average and smallest range scores value innovation and can support project goals. The survey, by design, skews scores toward the "agreement" scale. Use the following decision criteria to determine these scores:

- Below 3.0: no support
- Average of 3.0–3.9: marginal support
- Average of 4.0–4.5: supports values and objectives
- Average above 4.5: strong support

Score each value dimension separately (see Table 6.6). Carefully consider your interpretation. Remember that small samples will not show large average differences. If the averages are very similar for the two dimensions, then examine each statement score separately and estimate the range. Use the same logic for interpreting the two dimensions of the values assessment survey as that for the innovation comprehension survey.

Select individuals based on their two-tiered value assessment scores and their understanding of innovation scores for the project need identified. Understanding what a person values is critical to project success. The project manager needs to assess the degree and effort needed to realign perceptions. Finally, the third determinant of innovation success is that

Table 6.5 Values Assessment Survey

Statement Number	Instructions: Check the box that best matches your agreement (disagreement) with each statement	Strongly Disagree	Disagree	Neither Disagree nor Agree	Agree	Strongly Agree
1	The core mission of my company has my support.					
2	The strengths of my organization help me to accomplish my work.					
3	Weaknesses in the organization do not deter my enthusiasm.					
4	Individuals are committed to the success of the organization.					
5	Management effectively motivates employees.					
6	Applying positive values to the work environment is helpful.					
7	Accepting the assigned priorities for the most critical tasks is easy.					
8	My beliefs can conform to achieve the desired objective.					

(Continued)

Table 6.5 (*Continued*) Values Assessment Survey

Statement Number	Instructions: Check the box that best matches your agreement (disagreement) with each statement	Strongly Disagree	Disagree	Neither Disagree nor Agree	Agree	Strongly Agree
9	Empowering others is a value that generates success.					
10	Teams can frequently achieve greater success than individuals.					

Table 6.6   Scoring Guide—Values Assessment

Value Dimension or Theme	Mean (average) Range of Statements (largest to smallest value)
Organizational value	(Sum of statements 1 to 5) ÷ 5
Project value	(Sum of statements 6 to 10) ÷ 5

of a perceptual assessment of the work environment. This, too, is a proprietary tool that Global Targeting, Inc. provides to organizations. This tool and its analysis (provided in the next section) provide an assessment of the work environment and are available from Global Targeting, Inc. Results from these surveys create a profile of available candidates using a three-coordinate decision criterion (understanding of innovation, values assessment, and attitudes regarding the work environment) as a selection mechanism. The three-coordinate system, discussed in this book, provides an effective but limited method of team member selection.

Surveys measure perceptions. A perception is an evaluation of what you believe or think you have experienced about a tangible product or service. Perceptions are highly influenced by events and experiences. Once a perception becomes a belief, it takes additional effort (time, cost, benefits) to change the belief. Perceptions are temporary while beliefs are more permanent.

If your perception is that you receive poor service at a restaurant, then chances are you will not return. No effort or realignment will change your mind. The same is true for values. Therefore, those who strongly support values in line with the project need little or no realignment of their perceptions. For those who score lower, their perceptions need frequent alignment to ensure project success; a low score never disqualifies anyone, but can be a significant red flag. Never assume that a lower score indicates a person who is incapable of innovating. What it does mean is that the person needs his or her perception of innovation aligned to the identified need.

With time, perceptions become beliefs and individuals act on their beliefs. If someone believes that innovation is impossible, then the reality becomes true and his or her behavior will support such beliefs. A team of individuals with a different understanding of innovation and a different value system lacks adequate preparation for project success. There are numerous incidences where ill prepared teams were thrust onto a project that they could not complete. Often, the selection criteria involve experience, education, or function. As we have stated, these are minor criteria in terms of innovation. The selection choice must focus on the individual, as this is how innovation begins. In future chapters, we will discuss methods to align both expectations and perceptions.

Selecting the Team—Overall Perceptions of the Work Environment

The third determinant for team selection is an individual's assessment of his or her work environment. We evaluate team members using a three-component approach (comprehension, value assessment, and workplace environment evaluation). We want to know how a prospective team member perceives his or her work environment. The work environment consists of statements related to items such as trust, collaboration, creativity, workload, and problem-solving ability.

A cooperative attitude is critical for success. Selecting team members requires that management choose employees willing and able to work in a group (team) setting. Global Targeting, Inc. has developed a proprietary tool that assesses the work environment. Those who struggle with the work environment may not be a good choice as a potential team member. Given the sensitivity of this information, Global Targeting, Inc. does not release information that identifies individuals to companies or organizations, but it does provide an overall assessment of attitudes related to the work environment.

To assess individuals about their perceptions of the work environment, we suggest distributing the work environment assessment survey (Table 6.7), which measures three unique characteristics of the work environment:

1. Collaboration, challenges, and trust
2. Creativity and problem solving
3. Workload and rewards

Score each response with the score coding guide developed earlier in this chapter. Attach a numerical value of 1 to "strongly disagree" and a 5 to "strongly agree." When the data are analyzed for statistical purposes, this is the simpler approach. Of course, you can use the original designations when creating charts and graphs in Microsoft Excel.

The survey, by design, skews scores toward the "agreement" scale. Use the following interpretation guide to determine these scores:

■ Below 3.0: no support
■ Average of 3.0–3.9: marginal support
■ Average of 4.0–4.5: supports work environment issues
■ Average above 4.5: strong support for work environment issues

Score each value dimension separately. Carefully consider your interpretation. Remember that small samples will not show large average differences. If the averages are very similar for the two dimensions, then examine each statement score separately and estimate the range. A small or zero range indicates consistency. Use the same logic for

Table 6.7   Work Environment Assessment Survey

Statement Number	Instructions: Check the box that best matches your agreement (disagreement) with each statement	Strongly Disagree	Disagree	Neither Disagree nor Agree	Agree	Strongly Agree
1	The work environment supports creativity.					
2	I have confidence in my own abilities to solve problems.					
3	My workplace provides me with challenges.					
4	The workplace enables me to be creative.					
5	The work environment is open to new ideas.					
6	There is a sense of cooperation among employees.					
7	Management rewards improvements.					
8	Work demands are not overburdening.					
9	My workplace encourages change.					
10	Trust is valued in my workplace.					

Table 6.8 Work Environment Themes

Work Environment Theme	*Mean (average)/Range of Statements*
Collaboration, challenges, and trust	(State 3 + State 6 + State 10) ÷ 3 Range = largest to smallest value
Creativity/problem solving	(Statement 1 + Statement 2 + Statement 4 + Statement 5) ÷ 4 Range = largest to smallest value
Workload and reward	(Statement 7 + Statement 8 + Statement 9) ÷ 3 Range = largest to smallest value

interpreting the three dimensions of the work environment assessment survey (see Table 6.8) as those for the values assessment survey.

Obviously, you must trust your employees to provide answers that truly represent their feelings and attitudes. All-positive responses do not always identify the best team members. Providing an honest assessment with a positive attitude would also be a trait of an excellent team member. The process requires both empirical data and a good sense of judgment. Choose individuals based not only on experience or education but also on attitude, drive, and ambition. Do not just rely on the results of the surveys, as you will miss qualified individuals. Keep an even balance of empirical evidence to opinion and choose the best person for the project.

Many organizations struggle with administering surveys as well as interpreting the results. Our client, Choucair Testing, was excited over the results and their implications. The largest interests for management were the attitudes that employees expressed. First, the company's employees had a high degree of pride in their work and their company. Second, some believed that Choucair management did not always respond to these needs. Both of these findings resonated with Choucair senior management because they demonstrated that innovation success is the product of multiple elements working in a collaborative manner. Incidentally, those findings convinced management to fund this project.

Keep the Project Objective Focus—Ongoing

It is critical to keep project objectives in clear focus throughout the project, from design to implementation. One simple method is to keep the innovation objective visible by discussing it at every team meeting or presentation. Open every meeting by reading and discussing the objective. The NASA objective was "to land a person on the moon and return them safely back to Earth." This was the purpose and reason for the project. Obviously, there were many subprojects and a large number of subproject objectives. However, realignment or replacement awaited those objectives that did not support NASA's main purpose.

This may seem rather simplistic, but how many meetings have you attended (or even facilitated) where the objective was unknown or changed, leading to chaos at times. We need to keep the objective as our project "mantra." It is easy to deviate from the objective. We see opportunities for new applications, advancement for ourselves and our ideas, and overall improvement. Yet, this behavior causes serious delays and issues. Project management is as much about accomplishing tasks as it is about managing human behavior. The old adage that the best description of project management is that it is as if one were "herding cats" is very true. The team leader needs to be aware of the roadblocks and plan accordingly. We can only warn you about these potential problems and ask you to plan with these in mind.

It is not easy to keep individuals aligned, but it is critical for success to develop a constancy of purpose around the objective. At this stage, the team is only beginning to come together, so our warnings here serve as needed precautions.

Assembling the Project Team

Five key criteria exist for the project team:

1. An experienced project leader (preferably a certified innovation process leader)
2. Depending on the size of the project, three to seven members, each of whom is aligned in his or her understanding of innovation and supportive of project purpose
3. A well developed communication system
4. Time lines (milestones) for completion
5. Performance metrics

Require certified team leaders trained in the entire seven-step ENOVALE Solutions process for sustained innovation success. This process prepares the organization, function, and team for implementing innovations on a routine basis. In addition, we recommend project management training for all team leaders and consistent team membership for all projects brought to completion.

All innovation projects are unique. Team membership should include the project leader plus three to seven team members (for a standard project that would complete within 2–6 months). The team leader may assume responsibility for training team members in one of the ENOVALE strategies. Each dimension of innovation has a specifically designed strategy. Obviously, the choice of team members relies heavily on using the "N" stage criteria. A well developed and refined communication process is required. What this means explicitly is that there is a mechanism for communicating all types of information and an individual responsible for maintenance and reporting. Identify an individual to organize meetings including convenient recurring time for all members, detailed meeting agenda, summary of meeting accomplishments and next steps, list of recipients, reporting structure, mode of communicating (e.g., e-mail and an administrative process to handle deviations, etc.), notes, and amendments. For these specific criteria, structure is critical. Team members and management should be fully aware and supportive of the process.

As mentioned previously, our client, Choucair Testing, sent its survey via a link to all employees. In order to identify and select the best candidates, we hoped to trace the IP address to a name. We found eight individuals who scored the highest on the work environment and value perceptions. Unfortunately, we should have collected e-mail addresses to identify these people. We learned a valuable lesson: We keep the data to protect confidential information and provide only the selected names to the organization. As a "work around," we had Maria Clara Choucair, the founder, choose the 11 individuals who would attend the training. The individuals represented a large number of those involved with innovation plus a marketing/customer relations person. The key learning for us was to use judgment, common sense, and the data collected from the surveys wisely to choose the best individuals for an innovation project.

Aligning Perceptions

Experience tells us to select individuals with an understanding of innovation that relates directly to the need for the project. Their perceptions of innovation (how they understand the term) will align best with the project purpose. These individuals remain focused on the purpose and reason for the innovation, thus alleviating

1. Loss of focus, decreased productivity, and poor or missing motivational elements
2. Constant realignment to the project objective
3. Miscommunication, delays, conflict, and cost overruns

It is important to realign perceptions throughout the life of the project. Global Targeting, Inc. recommends posting the purpose or objective of the innovation project for each meeting, whether face to face or virtual. This keeps members focused on the objective. It is easy to deviate from the purpose and the consequences are often severe. Every deviation or misstep results in serious delays and issues that require time to correct. Management and the team must remain vigilant and establish a "constancy of purpose" regarding the goal as this will keep the team focused.

What if it is not possible to select individuals fully aligned with the innovation objective (as was our case with Choucair Testing)? To counter this difficulty, management needs to provide a compelling reason for the need (why the project is critical) and subsequent requirement for the innovation project. We were extremely lucky that Maria Clara Choucair is that leader who understands the necessity for placing the best people on the project. Her aim was to change the thought process and culture of the organization. We believe she will succeed!

When the individuals vary in their perceptions of innovation, work environment, and values, you can achieve consensus considering the following action items:

1. Formalize the need in terms everyone can agree upon and easily understand.
2. Clarify the benefits and potential difficulties.
3. As a project team, define innovation, as related to the need.
4. Provide a list of the anticipated benefits and consider any expected difficulties.
5. Demonstrate that the positives outweigh the negatives.

With the team assembled, achieve consensus (or at least agreement) on the reasons for the project and the expected benefits of the project. This will become the reason and purpose of the project and, from these, the project objective develops. The project purpose or objective becomes the team's "mantra" and a rallying point for its efforts. Agree to disagree, but clarify the need and the dimension of innovation best suited to that need (ongoing process). Reinforce individuals' perceptions frequently.

A Simple Example

Consider the following example. Suppose there is a need for a revised travel-and-expense form; this is to become the innovation project. Therefore, complete a statement that describes the need and defines the innovation.

> *Need:* a revised travel-and-expense form becomes an "improvement" innovation.
>
> *Define the objective:* to revise the existing travel-and-expense form to increase processing time, provide ease of use for employees, and provide information that is more accurate.
>
> *Selecting the team members:* Choose those who can align (support) this objective (i.e., those who best understand this dimension of innovation and value improvement as a worthy objective). Keep the objective as a focal point throughout the project. Once the objective aligns with its requirements, it becomes an outcome. The outcome then replaces the objective as a method of team focus.

Summary

A secret to innovation success is selecting and aligning individuals to complete the tasks. Using traditional forms of selection may prove inefficient and ineffective, given the information you now have on innovation. People will not align themselves without a specific objective and dedication to the project. This is similar to playing a card game, such as poker: Those with no experience require hand-holding, patience, and a constant review of the rules, resulting in slower than normal play and frustration for the experienced players. New players can

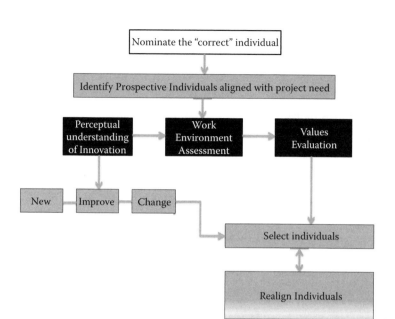

Figure 6.1 The "nominate the right person" process step.

frustrate experienced players, causing them to lose their concentration. Varying opinions and power and control issues all reduce effectiveness of the team and seriously affect success. Selecting those with similar knowledge and experience will reduce errors, frustrations, and delays. We propose the same is true for project selection, except that as the complexity increases, selecting the best team member increases success.

The second step in the ENOVALE Solutions process is critical for success as it drives an innovation project from an individual perspective. Figure 6.1 details the main components of this second step.

Discussion Questions

Consider a previous project objective that involved you or your organization:

1. Was the project objective within your span of control or that of the project team?

2. Did team members have direct or indirect access to information and resources?
3. Was the project delayed for any reason due to employee issues?
4. Were team members selected based on the project objective or for some other characteristic?

Consider the following:

- Identify an organizational or individual need.
- Define the objective and at least two to four critical requirements.
- What criteria would you use to select the best team members?
- Is your selection empirically weighted or opinion weighted?

Chapter 7

"O" Objectify

Introduction

The purpose of this chapter is to refine the objective (and the accompanying need) to create an outcome. An outcome is an objective specified by its requirements. Requirements are those characteristics that define functionality and usability; these are different for every organization and with every innovation. Requirements define the boundaries of use: in simple terms, how the innovation performs its intended use. The use of innovation is its intent (the objective). Therefore, for the 1961 President Kennedy pledge, the requirements consist of the technology, equipment, procedures, etc. and the performance of these elements to achieve the objective.

Outcomes are more precise than objectives since these refer to specific and possibly detailed requirements. The outcome is the rallying point for the project. The project team uses this banner statement as its "mantra." Outcomes are similar to a mission statement or guiding principle—a focal point for the team and the organization. Outcomes develop from objectives and requirements. One could begin with an initial outcome and then develop a specific objective and sets of requirements before formulating the approved outcome. At Choucair Testing, its founder, Maria Clara Choucair, gave us an outcome (based on a specific set of needs) and, from that, the company (with our guidance) developed its first ENOVALE® project (identifying an objective and detailed requirements). We prefer working from the objective and then developing the requirements to construct the initial outcome.

Just to clarify, an objective is an accomplishment, a goal is a completed event, and an outcome is an objective bounded (defined) by its requirements. Requirements directly relate to functionality and use of the outcome. Functionality is how the technology, product, service, or person will perform; use relates to its external performance, acceptance, and satisfaction. To better clarify these requirements, Table 7.1 contains a partial list segregated by functionality and use. The list is simple but instructive. Humanity innovates on a large scale for a reason: to meet demand and control supply. The limitations in supply drive innovation as demand continues. Because the need drives innovation, outcomes change with changing societal and governmental demands. As complexity increases, so does the need for more refined and specific issues regarding functionality and fitness for use.

Consider this example: Say that we want to improve customer handling at a call center. The need is for a more efficient and successful process, given ongoing customer complaints. The objective is to answer calls satisfactorily in less than 2 minutes. A successful call is one in which the customer is satisfied (use) that is executed within the 2-minute time

Table 7.1   Elements of Functionality and Use

Elements of Functionality	Elements of Use
Design criteria	Satisfaction
Operating parameters	Ease of use
Specifications	Efficiency
Job tasks	Effectiveness

frame (functionality). The requirements would include the technology, personnel, procedures, and performance criteria. All of these requirements (and more not listed here) relate to function. Use measures the number of customer complaints, satisfaction levels, and quality. Together, functionality and use define the requirements.

For the 1961 JFK speech about reaching the moon, the objective was a journey to and from the moon with the requirement of safety; the goal was to accomplish this by the end of the decade. The outcome was sending human beings to the moon and safely returning them to Earth before the end of the decade. Do not focus on the language but remember that an outcome is any objective bounded by its requirements (including assumptions and limitations). Even the noblest outcome could fail due to its inability to function properly or to find acceptance with a customer. Outcomes are what the innovation will achieve when meeting its requirements, assumptions, and limitations. From this stage in the ENOVALE Solutions process, going forward, outcomes will drive the innovation project.

Many will continue to ask where and when ideas come into the process. An idea is a creative solution to a problem. Ideas contribute opportunities for outcomes, but ideas do not initiate innovation—a need does. The prevailing wisdom states that innovation begins with ideas; this is true if the idea is described in terms of meeting a need. If the idea is a solution, then it is more a fix than an innovation. Innovations are more than fixes; they satisfy needs.

There are multiple opportunities for creative expressions throughout the entire seven steps. Tools such as brainstorming, affinity diagrams, creative thinking, etc. are all part of the idea generation process and are needed for creating outcomes. These and many more tools are available, but these are tools—not a solutions strategy for innovation. Since this book provides strategic information, we limit the tools, such as those associated with creativity and, especially, associated with ideas. The Internet provides useful information on creative idea generation. Although the ENOVALE Solutions process contains many innovative tools and practices, our intent is to provide a strategy for implementation only, rather than a list of specific tools such as those needed for creative idea generation. For now, we will continue to discuss the organizational strategy that facilitates innovation on a planned and controlled basis.

Outcomes

As stated previously, outcomes are objectives (based on needs) that meet requirements. Consider an example: Suppose you want to sell your home (a need) and recognize that the kitchen is outdated (the objective: update the kitchen). Before you undertake such a process, you would want to determine the requirements (cash, materials, available space, plumbing fixtures, electrical connections, estimate of time required, etc.). In addition, what are you assuming (you have the time) and what is a limitation (you have the money)? The outcome is the objective bounded by its requirements. Therefore, the outcome becomes the complete remodeling of the kitchen in 3 months without exceeding a budget of $15,000. The objective is for the project to be complete in 3 months or less; the requirement is to spend less than $15,000. The outcome states the objective, bounded by its requirements, assumptions, and limitations. Of course, the cost is the most important requirement, but certainly not the only requirement.

Assumptions and limitations provide a natural set of operating constraints for requirements. Once completed, management can review the outcome. The information provided not only defines the objective but also provides a preliminary review of its requirements. If both use and functionality requirements are accepted, then management can decide to initiate or defer the project. The outcome provides a tangible basis for the need. Once approved, an outcome quickly transforms into a more tangible asset. Moving forward requires an allocation of resources.

For the kitchen example, the next step is to create a drawing (specification) for the outcome. The drawing will show you how the cabinets, appliances, plumbing, and counter space will appear when completed. The drawing (architect's plans) visualizes the outcome by detailing how the requirements are used and met. In essence, the drawing brings life to the outcome. The specifics transform the outcome into a tangible item. Once the project begins, the tangible elements of the outcome become the controlling document. However, while in the planning stages, the outcome becomes the driving force.

Outcomes involve people, process, product, service, and technology. Outcomes consist of objectives bounded by requirements. Validate the outcome (objective, requirements, assumptions, and limitations) before beginning the project. When the outcome can meet its bounded requirements, it is viable. The outcome is sustainable if its viability is consistent over time.

Moving ideas to a concept is a more traditional approach to innovation. The concept is a design that visualizes the idea. Needs are often overlooked, and the concept normally does not include objectives or requirements. Traditionally, this information develops over time. The danger in this approach is to place too much emphasis on the idea before it has been sufficiently evaluated. Our experience has taught us that good ideas frequently do not transform well into a viable project. We use the ENOVALE process for innovation so that organizations do not expend time, resources, and efforts on an impractical project. Therefore, outcomes provide the information needed to make a successful decision.

Outcomes will drive the innovation project once validated, aligned, and linked to organizational performance measures. For each innovation dimension, a specific outcome exists. For example, for innovative change, people are the driving force of the outcome. People are not the only requirement—just the most important. By this stage of the ENOVALE Solutions process, it should be obvious why outcomes drive innovation projects. Outcomes are a statement of what the innovation will achieve.

Consider the following example. Suppose you want to generate electricity with wind power. This is a very admirable goal, but what is the outcome? The outcome is the objective (generating electricity from wind power) and its requirements. The requirements pose a problem:

- The device to generate electricity is large, obtrusive, noisy.
- It is dependent upon ambient conditions that are not practical for most homeowners.
- There is difficulty with maintenance and repair.
- There is a need for battery backup or hookup from a central source.

What appears to be a good idea is less than a desired outcome. The difficulty in installing, maintaining, and deriving electricity on a consistent basis makes this an unacceptable outcome and not a good innovation project. Outcomes act as filters to ensure that the proposed innovation project can accomplish its objectives. With time, the organization will consider outcomes as simple as objectives or goals.

Begin first with the most critical requirements; use these to refine or replace the outcome. Time well spent now eliminates redesign and redevelopment efforts. It also reduces the project costs and missteps so commonly found in most traditional innovation projects. For innovation project success, both functional (operational) requirements and use (customer or end user) requirements should relate to one another. This relationship strongly suggests that meeting customer use requirements requires that operational elements must perform to expectations. If the relationship is weak, then certain functional elements may be unnecessary or underperforming at this point.

Table 7.2   Outcome Refinement Matrix

Items	Use 1	Use 2	Use 3
Function 1			
Function 2			
Function 3			
Function 4			
Function 5			
Function 6			
Function 7			
Function 8			
Function 9			

For a negative relationship, the functional requirement would cause a significant decrease in performance, requiring replacement or modification.

The outcome refinement matrix is a tool that identifies whether the relationships are supportive. The purpose of this tool is evaluative; it establishes that a relationship between use and functionality is present and critical for success. It establishes a direct link between the needs of the user and the technical requirements of the product, service, or technology. The better the relationship between use and function is, the easier it is to achieve the innovation objective. As an evaluative tool, the matrix (Table 7.2) will provide information on the strength of the relationship between the functional requirement and the user.

Outcome Refinement Matrix

Begin with the objective and its requirements. Select five functional (operational) and three to five use (customer or user) requirements. Rate these on the presumed relationship

Table 7.3   Example of Outcome Refinement Matrix

	Customer or End User	Use 1	Use 2	Use 3
Operational		*Satisfaction*	*Time to Complete Call*	*Ease of Use*
Function 1	Technology	S	M	S
Function 2	Entry message	M	M	S
Function 3	Entry menu	S	S	S
Function 4	Understanding of menu items	S	S	S
Function 5	Transfer capability	M	W	W
Function 6	Attendant	S	S	M
Function 7	Information provided	S	S	S

(strong = "S," medium = "M," weak = "W," or negative = "N"). A negative relationship indicates that a functional requirement suffers (loses performance) in relation to a use requirement. Negative relationships require further evaluation. Consider the example of the call center that must improve its efficiency and effectiveness. The matrix in Table 7.3 is an example of how use and functional requirement relate to one another. Defining and refining outcomes are time consuming but necessary; how the outcome performs is critical for success. In addition, consider evaluating limitations, assumptions, and overall applicability.

Finally, ensure that the outcomes link to success criteria. Avoiding or reducing this stage limits the scope and will cause problems for the future success of the project. It is inevitable that outcomes will change based on the information obtained during the early stages of an innovation project. It is critical to revisit the success criteria from a changed outcome. Be sure to highlight changes in the outcome, as this is the guiding objective for the team. Changes require using practices such as the KISS principle, which says to keep it simply stated to minimize confusion.

A Simple Example

Discussing and using outcomes will take time to understand its purpose and the reasons why this process is critical for success. Consider the process of baking cookies (thanks to Maria Clara Choucair for this idea). If our present process allows us to bake and sell 50 cookies, it is possible to sell more without doubling our costs. In order to determine if this is a viable project, the innovation team needs to produce a viable outcome statement. Outcomes are objectives bounded by requirements. Therefore, brainstorm objectives and requirements to create an initial or preliminary outcome statement. Figure 7.1 details this process.

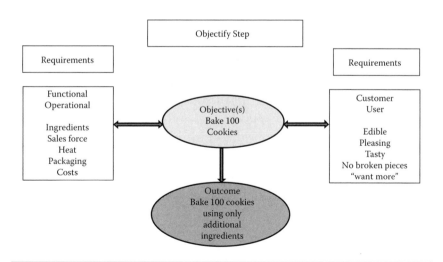

Figure 7.1   The objectify step: simple example.

It is an iterative process to create an outcome. Generally, it involves more than one objective and a series of requirements. The outcome can only exist if it meets its requirements. The natural question is whether this is worth the effort. Innovation projects are special projects that must perform beyond other projects. Our research has shown that poorly defined outcomes greatly increase the chance of failure. For the cookie example, the team did develop a single outcome to meet a desired requirement. The next step is to validate the outcome, which is the subject of the next chapter.

Summary

The most critical deliverable from the ENOVALE process is the outcome. It provides both an objective and a tangible description of what the innovation will accomplish. Outcomes provide a wealth of information on requirements and usage. If the outcome cannot perform, then its viability and sustainability are in question.

Some may ask, "Is this worth the effort?" The answer is clear and precise: We want the outcome (innovation) to succeed. Efforts at this point are much less stringent than at the development phase. Given the heavy influence of individuals throughout the innovation process, it is only natural that information on performance and use be available to judge the innovation's success. The more information offered and evaluation conducted, the simpler the decision will be. Simplicity is a key in any accurate decision making. If the outcome is worthwhile, proceed; if not, then either end activity or consider alternatives. The assessment of the outcome greatly improves successful implementation.

The third step in the ENOVALE Solutions process is critical for success as it evaluates an innovation project from its outcome, requirements, and objective. Figure 7.2 details the main components of this third step.

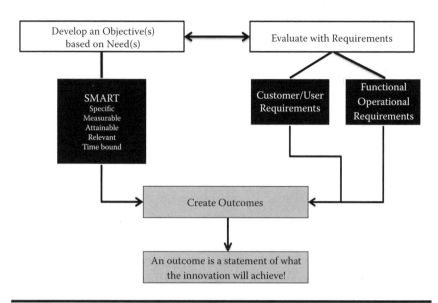

Figure 7.2 The "objectify" process step.

Discussion Questions

Consider an existing innovation developed within your organization:

1. Are outcomes derived from a specific need and evaluated for performance and use?
   a. If not, why examine the criteria to judge viability and sustainability?
   b. Did criteria exist to judge performance?
   c. Can outcome definition facilitate decision making?
2. Did the outcome list requirements and "fitness for use" criteria?
3. Were all objectives stated and properly applied?
4. Did the outcome consider the influence of people, process, and technology?

Consider a simple need for the organization:

1. Translate the need into an outcome.
2. Determine the critical requirements in terms of function and user concerns.
3. Objectify the outcome. Evaluate its worth and achievability.

Chapter 8

"V" Validate

Introduction

The most critical element in verifying the outcome's viability is through validation. Validation is the process of verifying that certain requirements, limitations, and assumptions are correct and functioning properly. Previously, we reviewed objectives, requirements, and their influence on outcomes. In this chapter, we broaden the discussion to include limitations and assumptions. This chapter presents a simple but reliable method and a tool to evaluate these criteria.

Consider the space shuttle *Discovery* explosion in 1986. The reason for the explosion and subsequent loss of life was due to a poor assumption and an unknown or forgotten limitation in making the launch decision. One limitation for the O-rings that sealed the different sections of the solid rocket motor was the lack of an operational test at freezing temperatures (since the Kennedy Space Center is in Florida and the assumption was that Florida rarely had freezing temperatures). Therefore, the failures of the O-rings after liftoff were due to a little known limitation as well as a violation of an assumption. The outcome was devastating and is an example of why we need to evaluate assumptions and limitations but also be aware of the potential for failure.

A limitation is that which prevents, deters, or interferes with performance. As discussed previously, performance measures operational efficiency and effectiveness: in simple terms, how well a product, process, or technology can function (work). Limitations could come from a process, person, service, or product resulting in less than expected performance. There is no innovation without a control mechanism to reduce the influence of limitations. Conversely, too many assumptions, especially those untested or given low priority, cause numerous developmental and compliance issues.

As much as we want to design and develop a flawless product or service, innovation without limitations is impossible. It is important to understand how these limitations assist in understanding the direct influence they have on performance. By their very nature, outcomes have limitations, and these limitations constrain performance and can also be a source of failure. For example, it took approximately 50 years to break the sound barrier for manned flight—a limitation with repercussions. Once broken, it opened a new frontier to faster aircraft, development of new technology, and the beginning of the exploration of space. It also caused sonic booms that were quite disturbing at ground level. This repercussion required additional creative thought and aircraft innovations to reduce or eliminate this effect. Understanding limitations and repercussions is critical to successful innovation. To help assess outcome limitations, we present a simple proprietary tool that enables an assessment of both risk and success (Figure 8.1).

An assumption, unlike a limitation, is intangible because its consequence occurs in the future. The actual consequence, though, is quite tangible and measureable. Assumptions are what we expect to occur or what we accept as truth. Assumptions are more difficult to measure, given

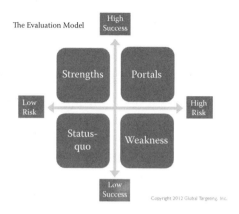

Figure 8.1   SREM: success/risk evaluation model.

their intangible characteristic. Evaluating the consequence permits an understanding of an assumption (whether the consequence does or does not occur) and its overall impact on performance. Assumptions derive from proven information (verified truths) or experiential conclusions.

The problem arises when experience and opinion influence or form assumptions. For example, no one knew exactly what would occur when an aircraft attained the speed of sound. Many people speculated that the aircraft would break up and the pilot would become disoriented, and some suggested that nothing would happen. In fact, the "sonic boom" was the result; few had assumed this particular consequence. Therefore, assumptions are critical; without empirical data, all that remains is supposition and conjecture, which are potentially harmful.

For innovation to be a success, it is important that we identify those assumptions made during the time of finalizing the outcomes. Assumptions are akin to expectations: things we expect to occur, given the presence of a particular situation. With all assumptions come one or more consequences. The consequence may be minor and of little interest or it may be major and have a direct influence on performance, fitness for use or product, or process or personnel failure.

Evaluating these criteria at a very high level provides a method for examining how the outcome could or should perform. Evaluating limitations and assumptions provides valuable information on both performance and success. If your organization has a formalized approach to evaluating these criteria, then use this process. If not, evaluate only critical assumptions and limitations. Once it is completed, use the evaluation as a decision tool for refining the outcome or replacing it. If the assumptions or limitations are too great in number (or too catastrophic), then reconsider the outcome as its probability of success may be compromised.

To begin the process, brainstorm a list of critical assumptions and limitations. Although there is no set number, keep the list as small as possible. Consider only critical assumptions and limitations. A list of 10 of each is a workable number. Rate each using its effect on performance. Remember that with each effect is a consequence. Use a simple rating scale:

- Minimum effect (will not affect performance)
- Expected effect (some influence but is known or controllable)
- Maximum effect (affects performance and is not controllable)

Do not overanalyze the result, but rather use it as a decision aid in regard to the viability of the outcome. Choucair Testing found the process of evaluating assumptions and limitations extremely important as it helped them to refine their requirements. In fact, this process may have numerous implications outside innovation. It is truly an iterative process (see Table 8.1).

Obviously, the time it would take to established limitations and define assumptions could be overwhelming in terms of project implementation. The intent is to provide those

Table 8.1   Performance Evaluation Table

Assumptions or Limitations	Minimum Effect	Expected Effect	Maximum Effect

who are conducting or participating in an innovation project with the opportunity of assessing these contributors to the outcome. We recommend that time be set aside to discuss major assumptions and potential limitations. It is not the purpose at this stage to eliminate the effect of all assumptions or limitations, but rather to identify and potentially rate their importance so that the chance of success remains high.

Evaluating Outcomes

The final portion of the "V" (validate) stage is dedicated to a structured evaluation of an outcome. An excellent tool for evaluating the outcome as a whole or its component parts (objectives, requirements, assumptions, or limitations) is the use of the SREM (success/risk evaluation model) grid. SREM is a two-dimensional scale using four characteristics to assess both risk and success. Each of the four-quadrant characteristics carries its own definition:

■ **Strengths:** characteristics that are easy to achieve (high success) and result in little or no risk
■ **Weaknesses:** characteristics that are difficult to achieve (low success) and carry risk
■ **Status quo:** characteristics that discourage opportunity (low success) with little risk
■ **Portals** (entries of opportunity)**:** characteristics that encourage opportunity (high success) with potentially great risk

Success is any tangible measure of value (performance). The scale for success moves from low to high (essentially eliminating a scale that includes potential failures). Remember that failure is a very different scale than success, so do not assume the scale measures both of these criteria. Risk is the chance that an event or action causes failure or loss (or further success and profit). Both success and risk have negative and positive connotations. As risk increases, it becomes more difficult to maintain a consistent outcome. Risk is not fully controllable or predictable and this may affect success in a positive or negative manner.

Evaluate each of the four categories on overall risk and enhancement of success. Before one measures success, it is necessary to define the risk and assign a simple level of impact to its consequences. Understanding the cause of a failure and evaluating its effects are critical. As risk increases, so does the opportunity for a more dramatic change in performance. The consequences of risk also affect use (customer acceptance and repurchase behaviors). As you position risk, consider its consequences in influencing overall success. Consider the evaluative tool in Figure 8.1.

There are three consequences of risk:

- Minor: minimal effect on success with small or no consequences
- Marginal: affects success and fitness for use; marginal consequences
- Severe: negative influence on success resulting in consequences affecting use, safety, and reliability

Given success's tangible nature, assign a value to it in terms of importance in measuring performance. As you apply the success/risk evaluation tool, be aware that increasing risk results in potentially harmful consequences (or truly breakout performance). If the risk results in marginal or severe consequences, then address the issues surrounding the causes and effects of the consequence. If the risk is minor, then proceed with the analysis. With a high risk and the potential for serious consequences, this further evaluation adds a third dimension to the success/risk evaluation model.

Risk is a characteristic often missed in evaluating innovation project success. There are industries where safety is a major concern and risk plays a vital part of any decision. Risk analysis in business applications is popular today, and this provides an opportunity to assess financial success. However, for the majority of innovation projects, risk is a misunderstood or a "back-burner" issue. Risk requires an understanding of the causes of and reasons for potential failures and the effects on success (overall performance). Find the causes for failure by "reverse-engineering" what caused the decrease in performance (and resulting consequences). During this evaluative stage, subject the outcome to common measures of success and risk using the SREM. Remember that risk can occur within any dimension of the innovation model.

The model assumes a relationship between risk and success (measured by performance).

Elements that define success are increases in customer appeal, number of spin-offs, simplicity, or cost effectiveness; be item specific. Success can be any tangible item linked to performance. Success represents performance over and above what we anticipate or expect. Success truly becomes reality when the product, service, or person meets or exceeds its expectations.

Using the Success/Risk Evaluation Model Tool

The design for this tool included application for use in numerous situations when defining the risk and success relationship. Simplicity should be the rule in choosing a measured scale for risk and success. Before creating a scale, define precisely what you mean by risk and success such that it increases (decreases) in a linear manner. For example, use the three-point scale (low, medium, high) as a means of using the SREM tool.

For example, suppose the team designs an innovation project to merge two departments into a single, larger group. What would be some of the risks and successes that could occur? One risk is a decrease in worker output and one success could be lower costs. Define success as increases in customer appeal, number of spinoffs, simplicity, or cost effectiveness; be item specific for your particular business or organization. For success, use the same three-point scale (low, moderate, high). Of course, you can expand the scales for more detail and specificity.

Consider the following example: Assume that a team is evaluating a possible outcome for a future innovation project. The objective is to sell 50,000 units within the first 2 months (this defines the success). The requirements are that advertising exist only on the Internet,

Table 8.2   SREM Example Success/Risk Scale

Success	Risk	Quadrants	Number
15,000 units	Age group not Internet connected	Weakness	1
15,000 units	Wrong age group	Weakness	2
15,000 units	No appeal for age group	Weakness	3
50,000+ units	Does not meet budget	Strength	4
50,000+ units	Product failure	Weakness	5
35,000 units	Does not meet budget	Status quo	6
35,000 units	Age group not Internet connected	Status quo	7
35,000 units	Appeals to other age group	Opportunity	8

the target group be females aged 24–38, and the advertising budget not exceed $100,000. The outcome is to introduce a new line of women's casual shoes (standard sizes) with heat-activated gel that massages the feet continuously at a price of $50.

The objective and requirements both affect success and risk and the eventual outcome's acceptance or rejection. Creating a success/risk profile table provides a method to examine risks and rewards. Table 8.2 provides an example scale and interpretations for the SREM analysis.

Remember the controversy that erupted when a particular cereal manufacturer claimed that one scoop of raisins was contained in its raisin bran cereal? This is an example of an unproven claim that was very risky. When someone decided to test the premise and found the claim untrue, sales decreased rapidly. Of course, the assumption was that everyone would use the same size scoop. Therefore, by using a smaller scoop, one could easily meet the advertising claim. Alternatively, using a larger scoop, anyone could claim that the manufacturer was deceiving the public. Be careful to get agreement on how you measure success.

Develop scales prior to outcome evaluation. Once the scales are developed, then outcome evaluation can begin. From the scales and SREM orientation, which of the four quadrants does the outcome best fit? Define what constitutes success (for this example, customer purchase behavior) for this innovative shoe design.

Each quadrant requires some form of consequence (either further risk or reward). Higher risk can provide better rewards, but at a price. High success usually exists at some level of risk. Obviously, if you reduce the risk (and resulting consequences) and increase success, you achieve a true "strength." For the example presented, higher risk is indicative of lower chance of success. Depending on the scale and your interpretation, higher risk could be more beneficial. In that case, a "portal" can lead to a breakthrough opportunity (where high risk is beneficial). Choosing the risk scale and interpretation is critical!

The remaining two quadrants are "status quo" with few changes and "weakness," which is an obvious signal for existing and future problems. Note: Global Targeting, Inc. has a more sophisticated proprietary tool for multiple evaluations, but this simple tool works for most applications. The one large advantage is that it changes the awareness process regarding risk and reward.

The SREM analysis for the example purchase behaviors and new (proven or unproven) approaches can yield an interesting set of outcomes (Figure 8.2). The SREM tool is flexible in its use and interpretation. Scales can change depending upon the need and the outcome intent. Scales do need to be on a continuum permitting incremental measurement. Even the best designs will have some risk and decreased chances of success; nothing is perfect, but this will highlight where monitoring and control are most critical. Even weaknesses and status quo performance possess opportunities. Use the tool in coordination with all other available information to make a final decision.

Figure 8.2   SREM analysis examples.

During the training for Choucair Testing, it was obvious to management that their original project would not meet the ENOVALE® requirements. It was a good selection, but oriented more toward improvement (fix a problem) than toward innovation (increase performance). By understanding what an innovation project entails, it was decided to change the project to one more suited for innovation (a project that would significantly influence the customer and give competitive advantage). The course participants used the SREM tool to assess the new project outcomes. Choucair Testing realized that the tool was extremely helpful in evaluating outcomes as well as reviewing and modifying assumptions, limitations, and requirements. In fact, Choucair Testing management used the tool to assess funding for future projects. Within 2 weeks of the training, Choucair had begun a second project.

The SREM tool is flexible in its use and interpretation. Scales can change depending upon the need and the outcome intent. Scales do need to be on a continuum permitting incremental measurement. For our example, there is truly no good choice for this product. Of course, many additional outcomes are possible, depending on the objective and requirements identified. Keep the categories simple for both risk and success. There is one outcome in the strength and portal categories; this indicates potential problems with key criteria (product performance, assumptions and limitations, requirements, or objectives). The next step would be to change (modify) the criteria to determine if a more favorable outcome is possible.

Many other evaluative tools provide information on choosing the best outcome and its key objectives and requirements. Consider the following:

- PERT (program evaluation and review technique) charts evaluate process flow and risk.
- QFD (quality function deployment) evaluates customer needs and wants and process or product requirements.
- FMEA (failure modes and effects analysis) is an excellent tool to assess risk and eliminate catastrophic failures.

Choose a tool best suited for the business and the situation, but *do validate!*

The Cookie Example

The second part of the cookie example that appeared in Chapter 7 is the validation of the outcome. Outcomes not properly evaluated are more certain to fail. As much as the objective and requirements help define the outcome, assumptions and limitations further define and refine the outcome. Finally, applying an evaluation of risk and success provides an effective evaluation (validation) of the outcome's viability and sustainability. Figure 8.3 provides the final steps in evaluating and validating the outcome. Of course, this is an example used to demonstrate the process rather than provide a detailed outcome for this hypothetical example.

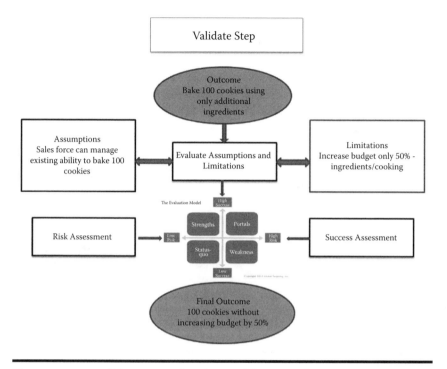

Figure 8.3 **"Validate" step for the cookie example.**

Summary

Validation is critical prior to beginning any innovation project. The purpose is simple: Be sure to examine the outcome from a success and risk potential. This will be time wisely spent at this phase and will yield payoffs in design and implementation phases. Applying simple tools will ensure that a potential outcome (and overall project) will succeed. Consider the large number of patents filed that will never see production or use—good ideas that had no interest or were incompatible with business objectives. Innovation is truly organic (emanates from the human level). Individuals are the most effective sources of information and the best decision makers for any project.

The fourth stage of the ENOVALE process focuses on validation. Before initiating an innovation project, outcomes

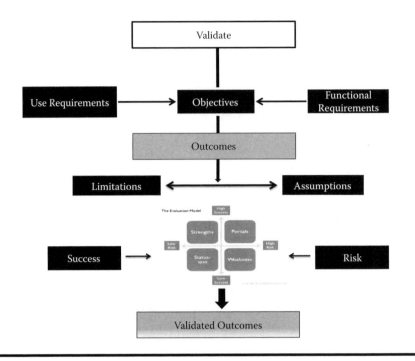

Figure 8.4 The "validate" process step.

need validation. Validated outcomes are the starting point of all innovation projects (see Figure 8.4).

Discussion Questions

Think of a good project that failed:

1. What was the main cause of failure?
2. What was missed in the planning process?
3. What should have been done to "save" the project?
4. Which part of the innovation model (technology, process, or people) was the main reason for the project's demise?
5. What, if any, learning was documented?

Identify an outcome that measures functionality, application, responsiveness to customer needs, etc.:

1. Use the success/risk scale.
2. Determine the quadrant of the SREM tool in which the outcome is best positioned.
3. Be cognizant of the high-risk, low-success scales and interpretation.

Chapter 9

"A" Align and Adapt

Introduction

Up to this point in time, management and team leaders have directed their attention to selecting individuals and transforming the objective into a project outcome. The team now prepares to begin the innovation project. In this phase, emphasis returns to the individual to prepare him or her for the project. The align and adapt phase works best for any innovation project that must reassess its commitment to and understanding of the project outcome intent.

There are two distinct but connected aspects related to project acceptance. When outcomes do not meet criteria, the resultant action is to modify or replace. That decision remains with management working on coordination with the project team. If management proceeds forward, then the resulting outcome is both viable and acceptable. Alignment of all those associated with the project to the project outcome constitutes the next step in the ENOVALE® process. This involves adapting the expectations of team members to the project outcome. Given the importance of the individual in the innovation project overall, these steps align the outcome to the individual's expectations and then adapt those expectations for the overall success of the project.

Before one can align individuals, it is important to revisit and reevaluate those values that the team members demonstrate. An additional survey is administered to the team members to determine if their values have changed and, in particular, the values that they hold regarding project success. Once the team leader understands how individuals value project success, he or she then can devise a strategy for adapting individual expectations to meet the project outcome. What is unique about this particular phase is that it will occur with every innovation project conducted in the organization. First, values are aligned to assess an individual's commitment to the project. Second, expectations are adapted and aligned to the success of the project. Team leader and management efforts to align and adapt values and expectations greatly increase project success, communications, and employee support.

Again, some people will say, "Why the extra effort?" Consider how many times you have participated in a team and, with time, the level of commitment and support decreases. Worse, with time, the scope and outcome of the project have changed or been modified—often without the team participating in the decision or even the discussions. This results in lower expectations and lower productivity. In fact, we observed that disagreements, disenfranchisement, and poor communications are often the result. Now, a survey will not prevent this from happening, but it will give a snapshot view of what people believe. Keeping individuals aligned to an outcome will greatly increase efficiency and effectiveness. Our clients say that this is a key point in achieving success. Teams that focus on the outcome produce more, resulting in fewer conflicts and disappointments. Vinny and I consider this good practice, but our clients say that it is a secret to success.

Values and Project Success

It may seem redundant to revisit values in this phase. In the nominate phase, value assessment helped to select individuals best aligned with the need to innovate. In this phase, the values assessment provides information on the team members especially as it relates to their continued support of the project. Rather than using the survey tool as a mechanism for selecting or removing individuals, it provides the team leader information to assess continued support of and alignment with the project outcomes. Administer the survey instruments (Tables 9.1 and 9.2) to team members prior to project initiation.

There are three parts to this survey. The first five statements measure support of and commitment to organizational goals; the next two measure individual support and commitment and the last three measure support of and commitment to the project outcome.

There is an option to readminister the first 10 questions, especially if more than 6 weeks (this is a suggested length of lapsed time) has elapsed. Administer the last five statements if you need a project-only assessment. Following previous instruments described in this book, use the coding guide (Table 9.3), the scoring guide (Table 9.4), and the following interpretation guide. Those individuals with the largest average and smallest range scores score the best response. Use the following interpretation scale to interpret corporate, individual, and project values:

■ Average of 3.0–3.9: marginal support
■ Average of 4.0–4.5: supports values and objectives
■ Average above 4.5: strong support

Remember that these are only estimates reflecting perceptions and best intents. Interpretation is subjective. The sole purpose

Table 9.1 Values Assessment Survey

Statement Number	Instructions: Check the Box that Best Matches Your Agreement (Disagreement) with Each Statement	Strongly Disagree	Disagree	Neither Disagree nor Agree	Agree	Strongly Agree
1	The core mission of my company has my support.					
2	The strengths of my organization help me to accomplish my work.					
3	Weaknesses in the organization do not deter my enthusiasm.					
4	Individuals are committed to the success of the organization.					
5	Management effectively motivates employees.					

6	Applying positive values to the work environment is helpful.				
7	Accepting the assigned priorities for the most critical tasks is easy.				
8	My beliefs can conform to achieve the desired objective.				
9	Empowering others is a value that generates success.				
10	Teams can frequently achieve greater success than individuals.				

Table 9.2　Project Value Assessment Survey

Statement Number	Instructions: Check the Box that Best Matches Your Agreement (Disagreement) with Each Statement	Strongly Disagree	Disagree	Neither Disagree nor Agree	Agree	Strongly Agree
1	The project outcome is easy for me to accept.					
2	The project, as designed, will achieve success.					
3	The risk of failure is small.					
4	My support will remain constant throughout the project.					
5	Any modifications will not change my support for the project.					

Table 9.3   Survey Coding Guide

Survey Response	Coded Value
Strongly disagree	1
Disagree	2
Neither disagree nor agree	3
Agree	4
Strongly agree	5

Table 9.4   Scoring Guide

Project Value Assessment	Mean (average)/Range
Corporate values	(Sum of statements 1–5) ÷ 5 Range = (largest to smallest value)
Individual values	(Sum of statements 6–10) ÷ 5 Range = (largest to smallest value)
Project values (project values survey)	(Sum of statements 1–5) ÷ 5 Range = (largest to smallest value)

of these short surveys is to assess alignment to corporate, individual, and project outcomes:

■ Question scores that all have the same value.
■ Do not rely solely on the score; look at the whole person.
■ Consider the source and the response.

From a project standpoint, you want individuals aligned with the innovation type and project objectives. Of course, surveys may seem to be "over the top" at times, but the issue here is support and commitment from team members. However you evaluate this information, make it part of any project initiation.

Consider those projects that failed due to miscommunication, infighting, office politics, and people issues. Spend the time choosing the best people—not just for their experience and talent but also for their commitment to and support for the project outcome. A good sales manager will tell you that support and commitment are the best features of a salesperson. If you do not believe in what you are selling, then you will not fully commit to the sale or the customer. Project teams have many of the same human dynamics as are found in everyday life. We tend to avoid the human issues, which leads inevitably to project efficiencies or failure. Do you need the survey? No! What you do need is a method to assess (judge) support of and commitment to the project.

Our clients find these surveys very helpful as they provide a "snapshot" of the person's intent and commitment. Rather than diminish their effectiveness, try the surveys with your next innovation project team. Discuss the results with team members and ask what they would suggest keeping that aligns with the outcome. Global Targeting, Inc. maintains a more sophisticated tool for those searching for more in-depth information.

Expectations

No, we are not psychologists, but we understand the need to keep team members focused on the project outcome. Employees have developed a series of expectations over the years regarding everything from salary increases to job performance to job responsibilities. Many times these expectations provide a way to anticipate the future and prepare us for positive and negative information. Expectations are those mental images and anticipations developed through experiences that we use to cope with life. When we drive to work, we have a number of expectations: no accidents or mishaps, expected travel time, expecting the building to be accessible and usable, expecting the company to be operational, and expecting the accomplishment of certain activities.

We expect many things and are often unsatisfied. Not having our expectations met can cause us to become dissatisfied or, worse, disruptive. For those with families, think of your kids when they do not get what they want: Tears, screaming, tantrums, no communication, etc. are what result. Do you think your employees behave any differently? Expectations are those events that we predict will occur. We all have our own expectations and these often interfere with reality. Challenges to our expectations occur when what we experience does not agree with our past encounters in reality. These contrast to perceptions that are beliefs and experiences tied directly to our actions. Additional confirmed experiences strengthen our perceptions, creating a template for future expectations.

We react to expectations based on the reality we perceive. If reality agrees with what occurs, then we confirm our expectations; if reality differs from our expectations, we question reality. Many times our expectations become the reality for us and, at this point, we lose the ability to support and accept reality. We all know the disappointment of some event not occurring in the way we planned. The actual reality can be frustrating and disappointing. This is why we both assess and adapt expectations of the project team to the reality of the situation.

Since expectations are outcome related, there is a natural connection to the project. Rather than examine each score separately, differences between expectations and perceptions provide the most valuable information. When differences are large, there is a disagreement between what is expected and what we believe. This results in lack of collaboration, communication, and conflict. Small differences indicate alignment of expectations with what we believe or experience. Table 9.5 provides a simple survey to assess expectations and perceptions and Table 9.6 provides a scoring guide.

Use the coding and scoring guides developed previously for the values survey. Be sure to identify those statements that measure expectation from perceptions. Perceptions are what

Table 9.5 Expectation/Perception Survey

Statement Number	Instructions: Check the Box that Best Matches Your Agreement (Disagreement) with Each Statement	Strongly Disagree	Disagree	Neither Disagree nor Agree	Agree	Strongly Agree
1	I expect the project outcome to remain the same.					
2	The project team is performing well.					
3	The project continues to perform as expected.					
4	Individuals are committed to the success of the organization.					
5	I expect my support to remain unchanged throughout the project.					
6	Team members contribute to the project's performance.					
7	I expect to contribute to the project's success.					
8	There have not been any major changes to the project outcome.					
9	The project team has performed as expected.					
10	The project is successful up to this point.					

Table 9.6 Scoring Guide

Expectations Versus Perceptions	Mean (Average) of Statements Range of Statements
Expectations	Average = sum of statements (1, 3, 5, 7, 9) ÷ 5
	Range = largest to smallest value
Perceptions	Average = sum of statements (2, 4, 6, 8, 10) ÷ 5
	Range = largest to smallest value
Difference	Subtract the expectations score from the perceptions score

we observe and then compare to what we expect. If there is a large negative difference, we get less neutral:

■ If the difference between the averages is close to zero, then expectations and perceptions are aligned.
■ If the difference between the averages is no more than -0.5 to $+0.05$, then consider the situation to be changing (i.e., in flux) either negatively or positively.
■ If the difference is less than -0.05, then the situation has deteriorated and a true disconnect exists.
■ If the difference is greater than $+0.05$, then the situation has improved.

A disconnect is suggested when what you believe to be true is different from what is expected. Suppose you make a reservation for a fine restaurant. You expect the meal to be good, given that it has received many recommendations. Revisit your expectations, once your meal is complete. If what you encountered was something different from what you expected, you could be dissatisfied, neutral (no strong opinion), or satisfied. Therefore, expectations set up what we want to occur; perceptions adjust that reality to what has occurred. If team members negatively experience something different from what was expected, then the overall effort will decrease. Add to these many negative responses and the overall mood and conduct of the team decreases. When perceptions and expectations align,

- The individual will support the project because the individual sees himself or herself producing value for and with the project.
- The individual will understand his or her role and accept his or her responsibilities.
- The individual will be satisfied with the outcome and objectives.
- The team will be synchronized for success.

Individuals who support and commit to the project outcome have an excellent chance of success. Involvement is the key for expectations. The more someone knows what to expect, the more buy-in the leader, manager, or organization can expect. Employees do not expect to be part of management decisions, but they do want to participate and offer suggestions. For successful innovation projects, keep team members informed about critical project decision points. Management (team leaders) can present a preliminary time line for the project including milestones, deliverables, and updates. Prepare a preliminary project plan or process map, including decision points, critical criteria (such as testing or evaluation), and risk assessment if needed. The simpler the document is, the better; people want to know the highlights, not the details. When a person knows what to expect, his or her productivity increases.

For example, an actor memorizes lines for a major scene in a play. The memorization and direction prepare him or her; they satisfy expectations. Now if an actor forgets a line (and all do sometimes), he or she can rely on fellow actors to provide the lines or a clue to the lines. The expectation is that someone "will cover my back." If the team is satisfied with key project steps, decision points, milestones, and deliverables, its members will react similarly to the actor: "Someone will cover my back." When members of the team know what to expect, they can feel comfortable with the future.

Team leaders and management need to provide a clear set of expectations for team and individual involvement, goals for each major project step, possible delays, and project "hiccups." Our experience has been that employees, when treated as adults, function as adults. The more that management integrates them into the planning and development stages, the more they contribute. Beware of the "glory hound" here (i.e., a project leader, manager, or employee intent on taking most of the accolades for project success). The team must share the workload and receive credit for resultant activities and achievements. Nothing kills expectations (and motivation) more than a person who is "bound for glory." Involve the team in both reaction and contingency plans.

Reaction plans contain specific actions, tasks, and procedures initiated when some form of failure (drop in performance) occurs. They are generally associated with safety issues, but for innovation projects, reaction plans are associated with changes in requirements or use (fitness for use) characteristics associated with the outcome.

Contingency plans are those actions initiated when performance begins to fail. These plans offer alternative actions or solutions to correct performance. Reaction plans "fix" a problem; contingency plans suggest different but effective alternative approaches. Require both types of plans during the project execution phase. Working these plans will not only improve expectations but also gain project buy-in. The best solutions come from individuals based on their knowledge, experience, and judgment. Identify potential failure points, project or material delays, and possibilities for errors; look for the hidden issues. If the team knows that a plan is in place to handle problems, expectations will not change dramatically. Incidentally, the same logic applies to perceptions.

Misaligned expectations typically exist in a particular business or organizational environment:

■ Individuals have separate and disjoint goals from the project.
■ Communications are lacking due to misaligned values.
■ There are feelings of separation or uselessness, blame and contention.
■ Negative sentiments and feelings do more to doom the project than delays, errors, or missteps.

To align expectations, clearly define:

■ Responsibilities, duties, chain of command—the events that will occur
■ What is expected of each individual—the behaviors that are expected '
■ How individuals will be communicated with and to
■ The mode of communication (for typical updates, for input, in emergencies)
■ Being honest—no project plan is perfect

Aligning expectations is not rocket science. You do not need a psychologist present to ensure that employees and leadership clearly understand their roles and responsibilities. Do separate personal (individual) expectations for project expectations. Communicate project expectations on a frequent basis (at key or critical meetings). Meeting expectations is also a useful task. Let people know what to expect and what the deliverables will be (and if a decision is required). This sounds like more work, but in reality, it keeps the team and project on task.

One innovation that a company implemented was that of revising its meeting strategy. Managers and supervisors scheduled 26 hours of meetings a week (leaving them few hours to accomplish their jobs). The project was a redesign of their meeting schedule, agenda, and procedures. Clearly stating expectations (what the meeting would accomplish) resulted in meetings scheduled in 15-minute increments. Total time in meetings went from 26 hours to 14 hours. (This is a great deal of time devoted to meetings, but it was a foreign company with a rich history.) Each participant received an extra 12 hours to complete his or her responsibilities. After a month, satisfaction increased, production improved, and the backlog was nearly erased. That is why expectations are so critical and important! Many times the simplest of actions results in improved performance and employee satisfaction.

Summary

This alignment phase or step is ongoing and is something addressed at every meeting. Keeping the outcome in front of the team increases alignment of expectations and perceptions. People aligned with goals and objectives perform better and require less supervision—the perfect recipe for success. We have found that simply by reviewing the outcome and communicating its requirements and fitness for use, we were able to keep expectations aligned. Team members felt connected, respected, and focused on the project outcome.

A more aligned workforce is better able to adjust to changes (adaptations) either with the innovation project or within the organization. Although most people do not like frequent change, when they are given the tools to cope, they can adjust their behaviors and activities within a short period. These skills increase efficiency, effectiveness, and employee attitude, thus lowering costs, employee turnover, and employee dissatisfaction. To accomplish the goal requires leadership and a common-sense approach. We are not suggesting an expensive company-wide program, but rather simple actions, such as focused communications (company briefings providing an honest assessment of financial health and the competitive environment, requesting and using employee feedback, and treating employees as adults). Aligning and adapting individuals participating in the innovation project will yield significant benefits.

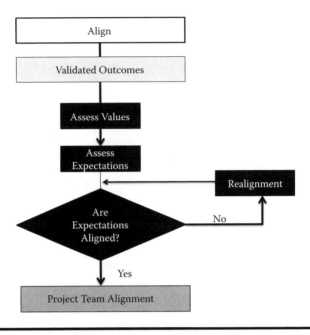

Figure 9.1   The "align and adapt" process stage.

The fifth stage of the ENOVALE process focuses on alignment and adaptation (see Figure 9.1). Determine what individual expectations and perceptions are changing and how they are changing so as to ensure project progress and future success.

Discussion Questions

How would you handle a group of individuals with misaligned expectations?

Consider the following:

- Look for commonality in experiences and beliefs.
- Stress the need for unity of purpose (support for the outcome and objectives).
- Determine the level of commitment and whether this could disqualify a person.

Propose a plan for keeping expectations aligned during the design and rollout phases (use the KISS principle).

Chapter 10

"L" Link to Performance

Introduction

As with any project, there is a need for performance measures. These performance measures are those traditionally associated with monitoring a project. Unlike previous definitions of performance (fitness for use, operating performance, performance to goals and objectives), performance for this chapter describes financial and project management metrics. A definition of performance does change for each dimension of innovation. That is, for an innovation project dealing with change, measures of performance may describe the effectiveness of the decision, efficiency, overall acceptance, costs, and overall benefit. Measures of performance will vary with the type of organization (profit, nonprofit, or government).

For innovation projects, performance must measure both viability (sometimes referred to as feasibility) and sustainability. For projects in their early stages, viability is key. Use whatever measures the organization consistently applies to evaluate the viability of the innovation project. The likelihood that the project will succeed defines viability. Viability includes measures of potential financial gain, estimated costs, return on investment, performance, assessment of risk, ability to meet and sustain customer acceptance, etc. Viability includes measures critical to the decision-making process. These will vary between organizations. The decision to end an innovation project comes when the measures of viability do not meet outcome goals or when performance goals are less than expected.

Sustainability, on the other hand, is a measure of success. It has components that are financially and customer or user driven. These vary from business to business. The purpose of this chapter is not to provide a list of these measures since most organizations or businesses are proficient in capturing, analyzing, and using this information. For some organizations, sustainability is the only measure of performance. It is unfortunate that most businesses measure some form of sustainability without first accounting for viability. This leads to projects yielding lower than expected results, increased failure rates, and excessive costs.

Beginning with this stage, the innovation project begins to take on the characteristics of a more traditional project. Therefore, you may ask, "Why the need for extra effort?" The benefits of a successful innovation project far outweigh traditional internal projects and therefore require special attention at this phase. With innovation comes change—sometimes subtle and at other times drastic. Experience with previous projects does not necessarily pre-pare management and the team for the innovation. Therefore, each outcome is different and requires different skill sets and a different approach. Bringing innovation into the mainstream of the organization requires multiple related (and often subtle) approaches to guarantee performance with each innovation effort. The ENOVALE® Solutions process is a standard for any innovation process.

Project management indices and software are all useful at this point. Global Targeting, Inc. assumes that success-fully executed projects are part of the organization's success and that personnel have the skills to manage and assess project performance. For innovation projects, it is critical to measure the "human" factor. In addition, the project manager must keep in mind that the innovation "touches" process and (product) technology. It is easy to see that innovation influences people, as they are the initiators (drivers) of innovation. Measuring the performance of people is as critical as measuring that of process, product, and service. In the past, innovations have been more of a technological breakthrough or an invention that radically changed the existing use paradigm. Nevertheless, individuals or teams reflecting the importance of the organic perspective initiated these innovations.

Performance and Innovation

For innovation to grow in an organization, management must be dedicated to moving past the status quo. This means that management must strive for and dedicate resources toward innovation, in whatever form it takes. When you work for a company that maintains the status quo, expect few innovations. You see status quo behaviors in monopolies such as power or water authorities. There is little innovation and only then when "nudged" by governments or designated authorities. Status quo behaviors maintain what is—without any emphasis on what could be possible. Implementation is slow and methodical. For example, power companies introduce new methods of power generation very slowly and deliberately. As long as these organizations can maintain a profit margin acceptable to designated government authorities, little change occurs. Businesses and organizations can do the same, causing a pattern of few innovations, with those innovations more a result of chance (i.e., special events). Organizations that plan, organize, and manage for innovation will have greater success.

Innovation can borrow many useful ideas, techniques, and tools from project management. However, innovation has a strong human creative presence, and this requires evaluation. The danger lies in assuming that project management skills will work flawlessly for an innovation project. These skills certainly help, but each innovation project is unique; it requires "out of the box thinking," with respect to planning and management skills to achieve success. Reducing innovation to a mere project diminishes its impact (influence) and its success ratio. The reason for ENOVALE Solutions is to provide management with a plan and specific skills to ensure innovation success.

Performance Measures

Performance measures vary from one organization to the next. These measures traditionally include financial performance, but metrics must go beyond these measures of success for an innovation project to succeed on a regular basis. Performance measures should include the following:

- Human measures (perceptions and attitudes, alignment to values, work environment)
- Time (delays, efficiencies, deviation from target, etc.)
- Materials and supplier measures (cost, availability, reliability, predictability)
- Process measures (costs, benefits, output, quality, etc.)
- Other project management measures, etc.

Each project may require its own set of unique performance measures. To use a set of common measures is dangerous since outcomes vary with each dimension of innovation. Always begin with the outcome and determine the best method to ensure success. Use measures of success for the outcome as a key for developing a performance measurement system. Of all ENOVALE phases, this is the most difficult since it challenges the status quo; additional measurement results in more work, increased cost, and more regimentation. Management can easily reduce or limit the emphasis of this phase, but the consequences can be disastrous.

For example, a large defense industry company was developing a new generation of aircraft. It was the first generation designed with computer-aided design (CAD) programming and software. Assembly of the aircraft was done in three unique, separate sections. When the day came to join the three sections, nothing fit perfectly. To roll out the first aircraft, the design team used duct tape to seal the poorly fitting pieces. The problem was in the independent design of the three sections. No measurement existed to determine how the sections would properly align. This is a good example of a missing measure of performance!

Each of the three dimensions or themes of innovation (new, improved, or change) demonstrates a unique set of performance measures. This is the reason that a standard set of measures, applied to each dimension, will yield less than expected performance. For those projects classified as new or inventive, require measures that facilitate the following:

- Idea generation and review (begin with the outcome; judge viability, usefulness, competitive advantage, business review, product differentiation, technological sophistication, concept, prototyping, profitability and/or cost)
- Assessment of success (achievement potential from technology, process, and people perspectives), feasibility studies
- Assessment of risk (what-if analysis, potential failure modes from technology, process, and people perspectives)
- Human measures (degree of creativity, viability, end-user acceptance, purchase behavior, alignment to outcome)

These measure elements of product, process, and people—all elements of the Global Targeting, Inc. innovation model.

For improvement projects, there is generally an established set of performance characteristics. However, even with techniques such as Lean and Six Sigma, performance measures are often lacking, resulting in a poor assessment of performance and less than desired improvement success. Most often, there is some form of measurement in terms of the process as well as customer (end user). Depending upon the specificity of the measurement, our experience tells us that less specific measures are often inconsistent. As we have seen, innovation projects require more measurement for evaluative purposes. Therefore, existing measures may not provide the level of detail to evaluate a potential innovation project.

With existing measures, ensure that linkages exist so that performance assessment is possible. To name the many measures and indicators that accompany a process improvement project would be impossible. However, management often overlooks or ignores one critical element: the employee. To ensure the success of any innovation project, include those measurements that evaluate human performance. Factual evidence says that 90% of future innovation projects fail without corresponding effective measures. This, we believe, occurs in failing to measure and assess the human element accounting for a projected 50% of the failures alone. Two human components discussed previously (perceptions and expectations) are critical to assess. Therefore, measure these elements frequently and assess the results carefully as the human component holds the key to success.

Finally, for the project that results in innovative change, the human element takes precedence. In fact, when developed, these measures would be useful for the other elements (dimensions) of innovation. Consider the following human measures:

- Environmental (before and after assessment)
- Resistance to and acceptance of change

- Attitudes (long-term perceptions) and expectations (the change may be viewed as positive)
- Repercussions of change (loss of productivity, turnover, cost increases, delays, etc.) that are negative indicators
- Benefits (cost, productivity, efficiency, etc.)

Rather, organizations need to consider the consequences and repercussions of change. Consider the following when attempting innovative change:

- Prepare individuals for change—communicate!
- Discuss the consequences and the effects of change.
- Remember that we all have experienced change in our lives, and most have dealt with it quite well.

Rather than fearing change, as many do, embrace change as a positive. When presented as beneficial, the change is quickly accepted and implemented. We all have experiences where change occurred without explanation or reason. Employees then spend their time trying to rationalize the change, adjusting, and adapting. For many, change is similar to the grieving process: denial, confusion, resistance, action (flee or stay), and acceptance. The sooner management can help employees reach acceptance, the sooner the losses (productivity, turnover, cost, emotional problems) will end.

Global Targeting, Inc.—Proprietary Measurements

Global Targeting, Inc. has developed a number of performance measures to aid in identifying potential project bottlenecks, problems, or inconsistencies. These are proprietary measures and this section provides a short summary of them. The variance to target indicator (VTI) measures the difference between planned and actual elapsed time. Its purpose is to evaluate project performance, assess the planning process, and indicate when deviations reach critical proportions. All projects exhibit variances, so the measure focuses on large or unplanned deviations. The reasoning behind this measure is to warn of potential time losses and identify elements that are causing undue (unwanted) delays.

The second indicator measure assesses project completion prior to project initiation (completion assessment indicator—CAI). Managers (team members) complete the form prior to project start. The indicator provides an unbiased assessment of project viability. Rather than initiating a project, only to have it fail later, this measurement performs a risk assessment. Based on various variables and the chance of success, this indicator provides a probabilistic assessment of success. It is one additional tool for decision making with regard to project viability.

Summary

Prevailing wisdom would denigrate efforts to measure performance beyond traditional financial indicators. Our advice is to take a contrarian view and invest in measures that identify and evaluate performance. This investment will pay for itself (its return on investment) quickly as it identifies projects that are unworthy of investment (from financial, customer, and human perspectives).

The sixth stage of the ENOVALE process (Figure 10.1) focuses on performance measurement. Link performance to the project outcomes not only for conventional assessment but also for those associated with human performance, attitude, and behaviors.

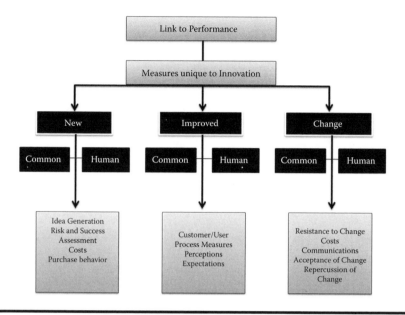

Figure 10.1   The "links to performance" process step.

Discussion Questions

Consider a simple innovation. Identify its type (new, improved, change). Brainstorm at least one metric. Does this metric

1. Provide information on both loss and gain?
2. Provide information on human costs beyond salaries and benefits?
3. Track viability and sustainability?
4. Provide real-time feedback and decision making?

Think of a potential failure:

1. Assign a degree of simplicity or complexity to the measures considered.

Chapter 11

"E" Execute the Project

Introduction

Moving through the ENOVALE® Solutions process, the final phase initiates the project itself. The innovation project, after undergoing extensive assessment and evaluation, meets its requirements from a product (service), process, and human perspective. For innovation to thrive, it must connect and integrate product, process, and people. This ensures that innovation exists and flourishes at the organic (atomic) level. Rather than a 10% success rate (described by Dahl, Lawrence, and Pierce 2011) after 2 years, success rates can easily exceed 50%. Our research suggests that success rates of more than 70% are possible. Those familiar with innovation efforts coming from a traditional research and development (R&D) environment will understand that a success rate that high is uncommon at best.

The reason we do not promise an astronomical success rate is that outcomes can change, causing projects to change. One of our clients, Choucair Testing, after working with us virtually, chose a project to prove how successful the ENOVALE process would be. The company chose an improvement project, but it was obvious that their processes (detailed so well by Johnny Candona) functioned quite well.

Rather than being innovative (with a defined need), the project was an operational improvement.

Maria Clara Choucair, the founder of the company, agreed with us that the project did not push the boundaries of innovation. In fact, she was concerned that the course we provided on ENOVALE would generate little value for the time invested. She and John Jairo Gomez, the chief executive officer, were a bit skeptical going into the training. The training kicked off as scheduled with an energetic, engaged, and very active group of professionals. The course was presented in English, as requested. The sessions were lively, with many questions about the process and feedback on the content and application of the materials. Summarizing the feedback provided three valuable pieces of information:

1. Put as many concepts as possible into a graphical format for better understanding.
2. Choucair Testing is a services company; developing and measuring innovation is more of a challenge.
3. ENOVALE is an excellent program and the results are obvious. Maria Clara Choucair stated, "ENOVALE is the first formal innovation management process I have ever seen." However, the process requires leadership and management for continued innovation success.

Our final day involved a review of the program. We talked with all the participants, and some of their feedback included that the training and the process were "groundbreaking for the company," "Participants wanted to apply the concepts to their jobs, not just the innovation project," and "tools from the training would help in setting priorities for future projects."

We validated the methodology and the approach (project impact research) with a company steeped in innovation. Maria Clara Choucair is a leader in innovation and she recognized that now a methodology existed to initiate and complete numerous successful innovation projects.

ENOVALE Solutions

Using the ENOVALE Solutions process provides the following distinguishing attributes:

- Needs are defined (from a customer or organizational perspective), and these transform into achievable outcomes. Assess needs in terms of functional and use requirements.
- Selecting individuals requires the knowledge of how individuals understand innovation, their commitment to project success, and their positive perceptions of their work environment. Alignment to the project outcome is critical.
- Objectives, requirements, limitations, and assumptions are evaluated for success and risk avoidance.
- Participants have their expectations aligned with outcomes and are "adapted" for the project. ENOVALE minimizes ineffectiveness, inefficiency, and poor communications.
- Outcomes are linked to performance that measures aspects of product (service), process, and people.

Without these tangible results, there is increased risk of project failure and the innovation project should not begin. The strategy phase requires that these deliverables be available. Missing deliverables will require additional time to create and validate in the strategy phase. The better prepared a project is, the greater its chance of success will be.

Final Stage

Now the project can begin with a high probability of success. Individuals align to the outcomes and can best support the project. There is a drive to succeed when the confidence level is high and expertise and work are appreciated. There will be less conflict, fewer delays, and better communication and coordination because of the alignment of employees and management to the project outcome, leading to success. Innovation does not depend only on project management; it also depends on the people who manage and participate in the process. The focus remains on the individual as innovation begins at this stage. E-N-O-V-A-L-E is a true solution, providing the framework for innovation success.

Next Steps

Understanding how to initiate a successful innovation project is the goal of this first step. Now the team leader and team members can embark on completing the project. The next chapter provides a generic strategy, appropriately called ENOVALE Strategies, designed specifically for the three different means of innovation. This strategy details the process of managing a project for a new, improved, or change-driven innovation. This is the ENOVALE process designed for training team members and managing projects. Rather than evaluating and assessing an outcome, team members actually participate in the process to conduct the innovation project.

When completing the solutions phase, the following deliverables are ready to implement:

- An outcome that is validated by its requirements, objectives, limitations, and assumptions:
  - Outcomes that contain reliable and verifiable objectives
  - Management understanding of what to expect from the innovation
  - Project vetted from many perspectives
- Team member expectations aligned to the project outcome (new, improved, or change), values, and work environment:
  - Understanding how a person perceives innovation

- Ability to assess individual values from a corporate and a project perspective
- Evaluation indicators that detail individual perceptions of the work environment
■ Established linkages to performance, success, and financial measures:
  - Performance defined and expectations established
  - Financial and success measures tested and validated
■ Estimates of project risk and success:
  - Providing decision-making criteria
  - Assessing risk and its consequences
■ Providing a pathway to success

The project is ready to begin. Without the information listed here, what are the chances of project success? We estimate that the probability of success drops below 30% without this information. In fact, empirical evidence suggests it drops 90%, leaving a success window of 10%. Certainly, organizational behaviors confirm this value, given innovation's "special event" status.

What if an organization only initiates 50% of the ENOVALE Solutions format or decides to do a partial implementation? We suspect that improvement will follow but not at the same rate as predicted. For it to be truly effective, ENOVALE must become a mind-set of the organization. Without an emphasis on the individual, innovation becomes a superficial concept that the organization can only hope will happen. Inaction backed with hope is a recipe for disaster. The completed ENOVALE process prepares the business or organization to initiate and complete ongoing innovation projects.

The next step is to conduct the project. Here, a strategic process leads the way to success. We recommend the ENOVALE Strategies process for all innovation projects. This strategy builds on the deliverables created during the first phase. The next chapter describes a generic innovation strategy useful for any type of innovation. This, combined with

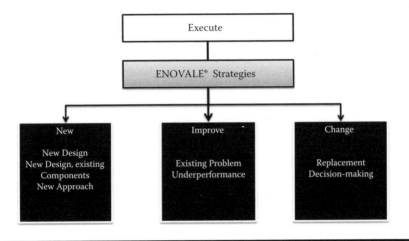

Figure 11.1 The "execute" project step.

effective project management skills and software, increases success, providing a blueprint for future innovation projects.

The seventh and final stage of the ENOVALE Solutions process focuses on executing the innovation project. Leadership and management have the choice of implementing a standard project management approach or selecting one of the ENOVALE strategies. There are separate strategies for each of the new, improved, and innovative change projects. Figure 11.1 lists these strategies.

Discussion Questions

1. What problems or difficulties do you see in implementing ENOVALE Solutions?
   a. Is it management related?
   b. Are there resource issues?
   c. Is it culture related?
   d. Is it mind-set related?
2. Which step will be the easiest to implement?
   a. Why would your organization find this step so simple to implement?

    b. What makes the organization so receptive to this step?

    c. Can this be replicated with other process steps?

3. Which step will be the most difficult to implement?

    a. Is this due to cultural issues?

    b. Is this due to overall resistance to new ideas or techniques?

    c. Do past failures influence future innovation projects?

    d. Is there management or technical resistance?

Chapter 12

ENOVALE®
Strategies—Seven
Steps for Innovation
Project Success

Introduction

Moving through the ENOVALE phases validates the innovation enabling it to proceed to design and development. The tangible outcome produced at the end of the seven steps can then move on to become a project within the organization. As a project, it will move from the design stage through prototyping and finally to completion. The process required to produce a successful innovation shares the name ENOVALE. Each letter represents the first letter of the word or words to describe some action to occur during the project management cycle. Strategies are those tasks, activities, and responsibilities that ensure project success. At this stage, the validated outcome moves into the design and production stages. The major difference between these two distinctive approaches to innovation is that the stage focuses on a successful project completion.

It would be inappropriate to select the strategy portion before moving through the solutions sections described in this book. The solutions methodology prepares the organization for innovation by treating it as something different from another management project. Moving from creative ideas to a defined and approved project misses the benefit of the solutions' seven-step process. We have all had grandiose plans that never seemed to make it to reality. How many times do we begin planning a good idea that lacks merit (benefit) and it backfires?

Consider the example of Delta Airlines' Song discount carrier. The airline wanted to create a discount carrier that could compete with the likes of Southwest Airlines. What a wonderful idea for the airline! However, the bureaucracy of Delta would run the airline. What happened is that Southwest Airlines was not constrained by certain union contracts; it was a very different airline. Song, on the other hand, was a part of Delta with all its contracts, agreements, and personnel. Flying Song was both fun and enjoyable. Unfortunately, Song disappeared at what would seem to be a rather significant loss. An innovation in the airline industry disappeared due to poor recognition that success would require a very different administrative structure than Delta had at the time.

Consider the case if Delta had used the ENOVALE Solutions process:

1. The need would have remained the same: a discount carrier.
2. Were the "right" people selected? Obviously, some were and some were not. Using what works for one situation (a traditional carrier) may not work for another.
3. Did the management team understand what would be required to compete with Southwest?
4. Did management validate the premise before launch? If they had, Song would have been a much different airline.
5. Were personnel (administrative, pilot, flight attendant, gate, and service personnel) aligned for this new venture?

6. Regarding the long-term fuel contracts that made Southwest Airlines so profitable—was the same logic applied to Song?
7. Did management leap before they should have to create this carrier?

With regard to Song Airlines, ignoring so much of what this book discusses is just one reason for this failure. Of course, many sporadic innovations have been widely popular and successful, but note the keyword: sporadic. We are unlocking a process that increases the success of any innovation. Some may consider that the effort required is too difficult and too time consuming for any lasting benefits. Good ideas can fail, leaving the owners with a negative consequence. Before embarking on an innovation project, be sure to use the seven steps of the ENOVALE process.

Global Targeting, Inc. has developed a series of strategies for new, improved, or innovative change projects. As part of this book, we are providing a more generic version of our proprietary strategy as an example of how to institutional-ize innovation projects within any organization. The strat-egy provided is usable with any innovation project. Specific concerns, related to each of the three dimensions of innova-tion, form the core of an upcoming publication. The strategy, although generic, works for any aspect of innovation. Each of the seven steps focuses on the key elements that need to be in place before achieving innovation success. Although this strategy does not provide specifics for each of the dimensional components of innovation, it does provide a blueprint for managing an innovation project. Realize that companies and organizations are different. Their needs vary depending upon their customers and users. However, there is a general strategy that anyone can implement to achieve innovation success. The key to success is to understand the order in which the steps must occur and the order of importance for each step to help achieve innovation success.

Each item and each company are unique. What the strategy yields are activities and strategies that ensure continuing innovation success. We cannot tell you how to build the next best mousetrap, but we can tell you what steps, requirements, and criteria ensure a successful project. As mentioned previously, the ENOVALE process is necessary for innovation success. Its purpose is to develop both a management process and a mind-set for organization-wide innovation projects. Once in place, ENOVALE Strategies provides a blueprint for project success. Although the first letter remains the same, the actual strategy does vary by innovation "theme." Figure 12.1 provides a visual representation of the generic strategy process. It is possible to execute some strategic steps in tandem to reduce overall project completion time.

ENOVALE Strategies differs in its execution from its solutions counterpart as a team can perform multiple steps sequentially. Global Targeting, Inc. is developing an "open source" program that monitors innovation project success, responsibilities, tasks, and project milestones. This will permit individuals to monitor progress and to maintain a history file

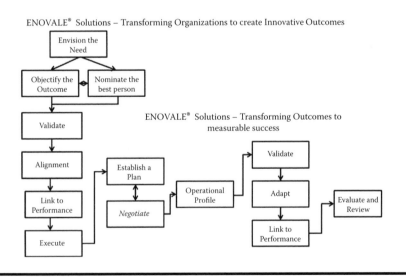

Figure 12.1   ENOVALE solutions and strategies.

and lessons learned file folder. The next few pages describe each element of the ENOVALE Strategies plan process with emphasis on application and usability. Each step will detail its own set of requirements, activities, and responsibilities, as well as identified deliverables.

Establish a Plan

Entering the strategy phase there are validated outcomes linked to performance and success measures. Alignment of team expectations with project outcome is complete. Sufficient reasons exist for continuing the project with an established benefit. Project approval has been completed.

Now begins the process of implementation. For a new or novel innovation (invention), consider any remaining unfilled needs. Needs can change or undergo modification by situation-specific events. For example, a need today may be simply a desire tomorrow. Therefore, reconsider opportunities, revisit creative approaches, and ensure that the need that drove the innovation in the first place is as pertinent as its original intent. For new projects, keep the customer's or user's needs in constant review. "What was impossible yesterday is often possible today." The most difficult aspect is keeping technical and engineering personnel in alignment with customer needs. An innovative organization constantly searches for unfulfilled customer needs.

The "E" can also have a component of evaluation regarding both the decisions made and the alternatives considered. When the process of decision making is more emotional than empirical, problems with the project will abound. Ask yourself how often "big ticket" items are decided upon by experience and emotion alone. Even common sense dictates that information and sound (rational) judgment play a major role in any decision. In fact, however, more than 90% of all business decisions rely on emotional and experiential information.

Yes, seasoned leaders have a great deal of experience and sound judgment, but emotions can temper experience. Do not examine each innovation through the prism of past successes as innovations are unique.

The unique nature of innovation requires a review and assessment of alternatives. With every alternative, there is a consequence. That is, no alternative is perfect. Assessing alternatives at the predesign phase provides a review of expected performance and its requirements. Now is the time to consider alternatives—no matter how small or insignificant these may seem. Yes, the outcome received approval and was accepted, but, as with every other product, process, or service, a second look can never hurt.

Evaluation and assessment are normal operating parameters of the creative process. Creativity is evolutionary—not a one-time event. However, many organizations consider this a single-point event. When creativity is examined under the lens of emotion and experience, it loses its uniqueness and originality. The natural tendency is for everyone to "own" some part of the creativity. Often the originality aspect of innovation is lost in favor of some convoluted final item that does not resemble the creator's intent. Keep emotion as far away from the decision process as possible. Many a great idea has been lost because of issues such as ownership, pride, and control. There is nothing more demoralizing than to have management or someone else take credit for your idea. In essence, innovation emanates from more than just ideas, leadership, or management; it begins and ends with the individual.

Upon finalizing the decision to proceed, the next step begins the process of establishing a plan. The plan is simply an outline of activities and responsibilities. Developing the project plans includes task, responsibility, and sufficient measurement (evaluation) decision points. The team can certainly use project planning tools and software at this point. Be sure to apply risk analysis to decision points and subsequent process steps. Our experience tells us that organizations and businesses have excellent project planners. Our contribution to this planning process is a validated outcome ready for implementation. Our project outcome is far more vetted than most projects, thereby increasing the probability of success.

With planning come activities, tasks, responsibilities, and decisions. All decisions carry a certain amount of risk. With risk come consequences, and consequences drive the need for alternatives. As part of the planning process, evaluate risk, consequence, and alternatives for those key results. The ENOVALE philosophy underscores the importance of the human being in driving innovation. Humans do err (make mistakes), causing risk and consequence to be part of the total picture. Therefore, good planning principles dictate the need for alternative practices, thinking, and responses (actions).

As the team begins to roll out the innovation, be aware of these natural and expected situations. We have worked on projects that have failed (been canceled) because one element of the project did not meet criteria due to inappropriate preparation, such as assessment of risk (often the chance of failure is high, but without adequate assessment remains an unknown), awareness of consequences, and lack of viable alternatives. What would have "pushed the envelope" was relegated to the trash heap. Several good, viable innovations failed because of poor planning, unintended consequences, or missing alternatives. In practice, we suggest an overall evaluation of risk (both success and failure).

Figure 12.2 provides a simple but effective procedure. First, estimate the chance of success, stated as a percentage. Next, assess the chance of failure, applying a percentage value. If the chance of failure exceeds 25%, evaluate the causes, reasons, and consequences of failure. Find alternatives that avoid the failure or completely diminish its effect. If the failure rate decreases, then add the additional improvement (percentage) to the success evaluation. The purpose is to raise the probability of success to such a level that the project is nearly a guaranteed success.

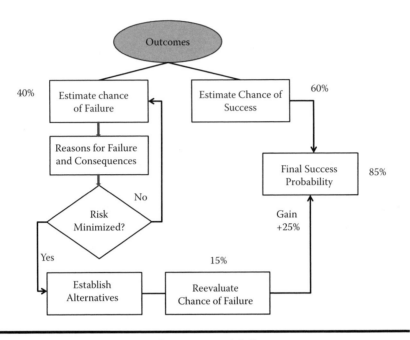

Figure 12.2   Assessments of success and failure.

Negotiate the Concept

This step can run in concert with the first "E" step. This step focuses on the process of selecting (nominating) the right individuals for the team. This can occur in tandem with the first process step. Following the prescribed process in ENOVALE Solutions provides a mechanism for team selection. Avoiding or sidestepping this step will increase the time spent aligning and adapting individuals. Many individuals—no matter how experienced, the number of degrees obtained, or their titles—do not work well in a team environment. Some work best alone at the individual level. Referring to an old African proverb, "it takes a village to raise a child"; so, too, it takes a company to produce innovation. Reward and recognize those who work best alone; use their expertise and experience as advisors for the team. Better yet, let them be a team of one. This certainly reduces alignment and adaptive time. Negotiate what works best for the innovation.

Since innovation begins at the individual level, creative people can certainly use the ENOVALE processes to achieve success. Allow creative time for individuals to produce ideas, outcomes, and strategies. Creative people will find an outlet to achieve, or they will leave the organization. Our intent is not to discuss the concept of creativity, but rather to establish the process of evolving the creative idea into reality. Management must accept the responsibility of "individualizing" innovation in whatever form it takes. After selecting the right individuals, management can then form a team and begin the process of moving outcomes to concept.

The assumption is that there is a tangible outcome: a new product or technology. For those outcomes without a tangible outcome (such as a service or a change in personnel), the concept becomes the decision and its antecedents and consequences. For a service, this would be a new or improved operation or process; for innovative change, it would be the decision and its consequences. The concept involves both the decision process and the resulting changes to the people (service process) affected by the change.

Once the planning is complete, it is time to negotiate the concept (or decision). The innovation outcome remains at the drawing board stage. It is more than an idea but less than physical reality. The outcome itself has become the objective and the decision to proceed. The concept takes the outcome and transforms it into a physical item (or intangible decision). The concept takes on the characteristics of an existing process, product or service, or personal tasks or responsibilities. A concept is the outcome transformed into a physical part or service, process, or decision involving human activity. For instance, if the outcome is basic transportation (remember the wheel story), then the first attempt at creating (visualizing) the wheel is the concept. Concepts are often drawings, diagrams, models, or blueprints. These are the first attempts to take the outcome to a more tangible level so that we can understand what will be involved in order to achieve the desired outcome. Transforming the concept is a human process. As with any interaction of humans, negotiation is key.

In any case, the concept evolves into a tangible (more definitive) reality. That is, the outcome moves to the concept and then to reality. Depending upon the outcome, the next step is to produce a prototype, a simulation, a first-piece analysis, an experimental unit, a proposed method, or a trial run. This gives the team the ability to examine and discuss the unit, item, or new method. Visualizing and touching (two powerful human senses) the unit is an excellent evaluative tool. Consider the skills a young child uses to examine the world; the child touches, tastes, sees the item from every angle. These are powerful tools. When an "item" lacks physical tangibility, such as occurs with a decision, it is helpful to explore the ramifications, to experience the emotional impact of the decision. However you examine the concept, do so with a set of evaluative criteria based on reality rather than on emotion or opinion.

Examination requires criteria to assess if the item meets all critical requirements. With sophisticated computers and software, it is possible to examine the reality in a cyberenvironment. Technology can produce simulations capable of describing reality. This may help as well to visualize or experience the reality. Modeling or computer simulation is helpful, but, inevitably, the concept must move to reality to consider its fitness for use. With time, simulations or models will become the prototypes. In fact, these computer applications can also provide a risk assessment of certain characteristics providing life data, failure rates and modes, breakdowns, and maintenance schedules. Resist the temptation to use only simulations or computer models as "reality." Nothing replaces the actual human ability to apply the five senses (and common sense) to the item, object, or decision. These senses provide us with valuable information that we use to judge a product, service, process, or person.

Negotiation is not only about the deal, but also about the process. Negotiate on the available information, tempering this information with experience and sound judgment. If the concept translates to a reality that meets the corporate needs, accept it and begin to implement. If not, the learned lessons are valuable for future innovations.

Operational Profile

This particular stage varies based upon which element of innovation the team is pursuing. In a generic approach, creating an operational profile requires an understanding of the purpose and intent of innovation and its expected performance and requirements. Performance measures can greatly differ from one organization to the next. Performance requirements range from simple to complex. Consider a specialty electronics component manufacturer who built and assembled components exposed for years (or decades) in outer space (they had to be very reliable as repair was impossible). The requirements were stringent, with reliability a top priority. Other organizations produce simple consumer products with a short life cycle, requiring sets of generalized requirements applicable to numerous iterations of the product. Establish expected performance targets and requirements prior to full implementation. As well, consider the type of innovation required and its unique requirements.

New Innovations

For a "new" project, consider the originality of the design versus its purpose. Three alternatives that define the concept of new are (1) completely original (all new com nents), (2) new design (existing components), and (approach (new uses for the product, service, techno or process).

For completely original additional designs, operational concerns involve proprietary information, security, secrecy, and protection. The rapid movement from design to concept is critical. The concept must become a physical reality (tangible) to continue the evaluation process. As the concept moves to prototyping, requirements, assumptions, and limitations become a physical reality. Operationalize the prototype to begin the process of resource acquisition, assembly, and test.

Begin with high-level development of outcomes. Part of the design process includes the formalization of operational and end user requirements. Remember that requirements remain tightly connected to needs. As the team develops the requirements, it may also consider the assumptions and limitations, which may be nonexistent in the early stages of development. In this case, the design must serve many purposes.

For a new design (using existing components), the operational profile should include potential patent infringements, product and technology research, and consumer buying behavior. These added requirements are needed to evaluate performance correctly. Consider these questions:

1. How much of the product, technology, process, or service requires new components?
2. Is it possible to use a large majority of existing components to achieve the desired result?
3. What employee or user skills need upgrading with respect to innovation?

The operational profile focuses on performance, resources, components, and people issues associated with the outcome.

For a new approach, differentiation is a key requirement as well as customer or user perception. Originality is limited to "new" features or applications. The producer or provider must stress a unique feature of the product, service, or technology. Shelf life is short, and competition can easily copy the ·ew approach. Place special emphasis on requirements that act as key differentiators. Choosing characteristics of the item related to requirements that cannot easily be copied is the key to success.

Do not confuse a new approach with improvement. The new approach meets an unfulfilled need (an unrealized need), whereas improvement focuses on improving performance. Improvement meets existing needs by increasing the performance in delivering these needs.

Improvement

For improvement, the focus is on performance. Assess performance at a baseline level. If performance is at expected levels, then innovation will increase performance. The need is to increase performance (however it is measured). For many organizations, such as nonprofits and governmental agencies, profit is not a measure of performance. For these organizations, performance can be improvements in efficiency, effectiveness, cost reduction, user satisfaction, etc. Do not let the word "performance" mislead, as the ultimate goal is to achieve measurable (and sustainable) success.

Improve only what is underperforming. If performance is less than expected due to an identified problem, then the process is to eliminate (fix) the problem. The operational profile (outcome) takes on the goal of improving performance. If the objective is to fix the problem, then determine the causes for the problem. Use other techniques such as Six Sigma and Lean to fix what is broken. Identify those components (elements) that can perform better. Evaluate the requirements for improvement (what increases performance) and set a realistic goal for improvement. For underperformance, consider the following questions:

1. What components are underperforming?
2. Why are they underperforming?
3. What are the reasons for the underperformance?

4. What is the effect of underperformance?
5. How much does the underperformance affect the bottom line?
6. Is underperformance consistent or erratic?

When performance needs improvement, ENOVALE Strategies provides a road map for success.

Improving the performance of the outcome becomes the focus of the project such that customers or users will recognize the improvement as innovative. That is, if the performance exceeds what is expected, purchase behavior or overall satisfaction will increase.

Innovative Change

Organizations have dealt with change since their inception. Especially today, strategies for organizational change are synonymous with success and competitive advantage (Goksoy, Ozsoy, and Vayvay 2012). Organizational change is those activities, driven by external conditions, initiated to modify behaviors. That is, successful organizations must constantly reinvent themselves to meet the needs of customers and users. Change becomes a fundamental building block of a successful organization.

Innovation is a key business initiative (strategy) to maintain or improve performance and competitive advantage (Preziosi, McLaughlin, and McLaughlin 2004). It shares the same essential goals (outcomes) as those strategies for organization change. Organizational change is a strategic initiative, whereas innovative change is change on a functional level.

With innovative change, outcomes directly affect personnel, process, and procedure. The result of change is a positive, neutral, or negative outcome. When the outcome is positive, it is "innovative change." For most, change elicits fear and anxiety. Given the natural inclination of individuals to resist change that is experienced in most organizations, the majority of change decisions result in failed outcomes. A 2008 *McKinsey Quarterly* study, entitled "The Inconvenient Truth about Change Management," found that nearly 70% of changes failed in organizations (Keller and Aiken 2009).

Such high failure rates are one reason why individuals resist change and do not consider it innovative. The focus for innovative change is to increase the number of positive outcomes. The key to change is the decision that initiates the action and, from the action, the outcome.

For innovative change, the operational profile is to determine the requirements affecting the proposed change. Its main purpose is to evaluate the consequences of change on those most affected by the change. Consider personal issues related to the change:

1. Existing employees (consider Maslow's hierarchy of needs), attitude, and motivation
2. Existing structures, budgets, and policies
3. Reporting structures and the personnel chart
4. Productivity (both individual and department)
5. Issues such as trust and value
6. Perceived value of change

Outcomes are the direct results of a decision, which is a key contributor to success or failure. Innovative change examines the decision process that initiates the change and the resulting outcome. How the decision-making process functions is a telltale sign of success or failure.

For innovative change, consider how the decision affects what is expected. Expected (future) outcomes, behaviors, and consequences change and guide the decision-making process. The resultant effect of the change should be consistency and a return to order and stability. Be sure to stress the benefits of the change, as these benefits are direct outcomes.

The operational profile stage varies depending upon the innovation element (dimension). In all cases, outcomes are developed and preliminarily evaluated. Our best analogy is "putting flesh on the bones" as you take a desired outcome and develop the reasons for innovation and its intended benefits.

Validate Performance

A consistent theme throughout validating performance is critical for success: Frequent and unique forms of performance measurement will increase the chance of success. Yes, financial performance is key for a profit-generating organization, but other measures of performance related to process, product or service, and people are critical. The example of "New" Coke comes to mind.

> After building up a 60% market share right after World War II, Coke was down to just 24% by 1980, due to competition from Pepsi. Pepsi was beating Coke in grocery stores, but Coke remained number 1 through vending machine and fast food restaurant sales.
>
> Coca-Cola responded to the challenge by reformulating Coke, based on taste tests against Pepsi and original Coke. New Coke launched April 23, 1985. At first, it got a warm reception. But pretty soon, letters began pouring into Coca-Cola's Atlanta headquarters, expressing disappointment and even hatred of New Coke. The company's hotline went from 400 calls a day to 1,500 calls. A psychiatrist hired to listen to the calls said people sounded like they had lost a family member.
>
> Old Coke was reintroduced as Coca-Cola Classic in early July, less than 3 months after New Coke's debut. Classic immediately outsold Pepsi and New Coke. The real problem with New Coke was simply that it was different. People wanted what they liked,

and it was not New Coke. Coca-Cola's marketing called it "The Real Thing." It is hard to change the taste of a product that your customers think of as "the real thing."

After the whole mess was over, a Coke executive summed it up this way: "The simple fact is that all the time and money and skill poured into consumer research on the new Coca-Cola could not measure or reveal the deep and abiding emotional attachment to original Coca-Cola felt by so many people." (S&A Digest, July 24, 2012).

This is an example found in nearly every marketing text because it shows that executives at Coke did not consider all critical performance measures. (Their outcomes were flawed.) Coke drinkers wanted the taste they had come to expect and enjoy and, when it was not available, they (and their money) fled Coke. Although Coca-Cola did run its famous taste tests, the decision to stop production on the old formula and proceed with the new one was made before evaluating this valuable measure.

For this strategy phase or step, validate with performance measures that reflect the product, service, process, and people, since these are true foundational elements for innovation. Performance measures can be simple or complex; generally, the simple measures provide more usable but less precise data. In addition, these measures provide performance data outside engineering requirements or profit targets. If the taste tests done by Coca-Cola were more than just a marketing tool, the information would have told them that taste was a critical measure of performance (product acceptance).

For those new means of innovation, validate the alternatives. Since performance is unknown but assumed, this stage validates the expected (hypothesized) performance. Validation affects consistency and predictability of performance. For improved projects, validate those measures used to evaluate the performance. It is not enough to measure performance; those measures must be validated. Faulty measures produce faulty performance indicators. Finally, for innovative change, validate consequences and alternatives. Investigate irregularities and issues related to the decision. Moving forward with a decision without examining its repercussions leads to failure. This will challenge the status quo that empowers management to make decisions based on feelings, experience, and past behaviors. Making the decision without first validating the consequences, hoping for good fortune, is foolish. Yes, luck can work in your favor and a positive outcome can prevail. With failures running greater than 70%, however, is it worth the chance? You have the choice to make a decision (for change) that results in innovative outcomes.

For those comfortable with the ENOVALE Solutions process, these performance measures come easily; for those not familiar with this process, it could be difficult to convince management that performance is more than costs and profits. It measures user and customer acceptance, purchase behavior, and overall satisfaction.

Align or Adapt

Alignment becomes a central issue at the start of a project and continues through completion. Failure to address alignment causes a breakdown in the team's ability to focus on the overriding outcome. Misalignment occurs when failures go unchecked. Misalignment causes serious issues with communications, collaboration, and progress. We have all experienced meetings or gatherings where a sense of purpose did not exist (or was quickly lost over a short period). The resulting frustration, disengagement, and ineffectiveness destroyed any benefit the meeting may have produced. All projects need a defined purpose or reason (rationale) for existence. Given project approval, continued alignment of purpose is critical.

Aligning individuals can be as simple as reiterating the project outcome or objective on a recurring basis; it can be complex if the team is virtual, covering many cultures and backgrounds. Continued alignment is an ongoing responsibility of the team leader (or manager). Expectations must be consistent across and among team members for alignment to occur. Revisiting the section from ENOVALE Solutions may be helpful.

Aligning to reality is a third component of this stage. New or novel products, services, or processes must meet a reality check. The reality check is that which complies with the customer's or user's needs or desires. In the end, the customer dictates success (reality) and what meets customer needs drives profitability. Consider as an example the following Six Sigma story with issues on alignment and on reality.

A major corporation (name withheld) wanted to institute an improvement project at headquarters. They assembled a team, trained the individuals, and began the process of choosing a project. No one could agree on a corporate project needing improvement. The team wrestled with a choice and finally arrived at an improvement project that everyone could acknowledge. The improvement project was to increase the number of blueberries in the blueberry muffins served in the cafeteria. Does something seem wrong here? Is a reality check needed? Can you not find a process that needs improvement at headquarters? Are these some of the most highly paid people, working on a meaningless and menial project? Management cancelled the project as soon as they "got a whiff of the blueberries." In addition to a reality issue, there was serious misalignment between team members. No one could decide on an effective project objective, so the outcome was a menial fix. Interestingly, the cafeteria staff, who baked the muffins, were never involved—a further misalignment. The point of this: do not underestimate alignment!

The same is true for aligning to a final decision. Expect positive and negative reactions by aligning individuals to the change initiated. Adaptation prepares individuals to embrace and support the decision. Adapting the organization may seem unnecessary, but with any new product, process, or person, the organization needs adjustment time. Adjusting to the innovation increases its success by improving the buy-in from employees, customers, and users. It is similar to the adjustments made to employee expectations. Even with negative change, consequences and repercussions are manageable, with quick dissipation of adverse effects.

It may sound rather foolish to plan to adapt the organization, customer, or user to the innovation, but remember that we know that innovation flows from the individual. Therefore, people need to feel comfortable with the innovation while experiencing its benefits. We recommend that organizations "sell" (market) from the concept phase. Efforts begun to introduce the concept will facilitate overall acceptance and support, both of which are critical for success. Marketing and Advertising can begin to inform people that change is imminent. This also provides the designer, developers, and improvement experts time to evaluate the product's performance.

Adaptation planning comes from an internal and external set of concerns and learning. Internal adaptation supports efficiency and troubleshooting; external adaptation supports a user and customer perspective. From an innovation item perspective, the adaptation phase provides time for any corrections, modifications, or errors before finalizing a final set of requirements. Test, evaluate, and review how the adaptations have added to the performance of innovation with regard to its requirements. This pass/fail step is a key for success as the innovation concept becomes reality.

Finally, for improvement projects, analysis is critical. The analyze stage assesses cause and effect impacts on performance. Analysis is not only data collection but also interpretation, testing, and validation. Analyzing underperformance or those causes that inhibit improved performance identifies opportunities for improvement. Analysis covers everything from simple data descriptive analysis to complex statistical solutions. Analysis of the data provides validation results and prediction. Data analysis involves both art and science. It is not only the software needed to analyze data but also the equally skilled and experienced interpreter to judge its usefulness. This stage involves not just collecting data but also methods to establish ongoing data collection for monitoring purposes.

Link to Final Performance Measures

As the innovation moves from concept to reality, a final assessment of performance is completed. Those who have worked with innovations over many years often recognize opportunities in the final stages of concept development. It is only human nature to want to feel comfortable with something that is new or better (improved) or changed from what previously existed.

The previous section described the need for adapting to human needs, wants, or desires. It is no different with quantifiable measures because we want these to be accurate and consistent over time. So much of our world operates on a single point measurement, rather than integrated measures that define reality. Relying on a single point measure is dangerous. Consider blood pressure cuffs that, if misplaced, can give extremely erroneous readings. This is why your doctor normally repeats a blood pressure reading given the inconsistency of the instrument and patient.

Take the example of the Eastern Airlines Lockheed L1011 Tri-Star that crashed in the Everglades on December 29, 1972. The problem was that this sophisticated airplane was losing altitude and the captain's altimeter was reading the plane's altitude incorrectly. The copilot's reading was correct, but the captain trusted only his altimeter. When the captain realized the problem, the airplane was only feet above the Everglades and could not recover altitude. Single-point measurements can be misleading. Of course, the accident was the result not only of poor measurement but also of poor communication and control issues. Given our convoluted and integrated world, single-point measurements provide only a one-dimensional view of performance. This is why we use the word "link" to indicate that measurements are truly integrated and require higher order interpretation.

This step is critical for performance and profit, but one that is missed or oversimplified. Think of the effort we take to ensure that our appearance is "just right" before an important event. We use the mirror and other means to assess (measure) our appearance. We know the picture we want to see in the mirror. Consider the same time wisely spent on evaluating the measures used to evaluate innovation performance. As one final example, in the early days of satellites, NASA and the National Weather Service launched a satellite to examine atmospheric patterns from a high earth orbit. The first pictures transmitted, using a specially designed TV camera, were spectacular; it was the first time that humans were able to examine their planet from such a high altitude. The satellite rotated continuously and, with each rotation, broadcast a picture back to Earth. The problem was that no one considered that a spinning satellite would see both the Earth and space as it spun. It did this and more—it aligned itself with the Sun, burning out the camera. No one gave this a thought in the design and development phase. It was a failure to consider the consequences and truly understand what the TV camera would observe.

Link to performance measures—not just profit and loss indicators. Obviously, with sophisticated measurement items, the results are more complex and interrelated. Performance extends outside the mechanical or process world into that which satisfies users or customers. Measures vary from service to technology and take on characteristics from numeric to perception. When performance measures for a product, service, or even person provide useful and accurate information, improvement (even a small one) can greatly extend the life cycle. Measurement is a key for sustained success.

Evaluation and Release

The final phase includes a full evaluation from idea to design, design to concept, and concept to reality. Rather than focusing on each phase or step as if it were independent, consider the whole as integrated. By implementing the ENOVALE strategy, which integrates those critical elements required for success, the organization greatly increases its chances for success. Evaluation is an audit-like mechanism that reviews critical elements. These elements define fitness for use. Most organizations have never conducted an integrated evaluation while implementing each step (phase). Most take the perspective that each step exists as an independent element. Yet, no product, technology, or person operates independently; everything is dependent. This is what this stage entails: the ability to examine the innovation from a holistic (a sum of its parts) approach.

This holistic approach is missing with many projects, especially unique innovations with little or no history. Inevitably, evaluation begins the item history; this may be of great importance in the future. Unexpected failures, breakdowns, or loss of performance are traceable to some event—an event that now has a documented history. Do not evaluate a single component or element, but rather look at the innovation as a holistic set of interconnected elements.

Finally, it is time to create release criteria. This is a final set of requirements and performance measures validating the innovation as complete and successful. These criteria will serve multiple purposes (final inspection, future audits, basis for instructions or guidelines, problem checklists, and troubleshooting guide). Their value is immeasurable; information is detailed and specific.

Summary

The strategies presented are generic. Global Targeting, Inc. has developed and validated a set of proprietary and detailed implementation strategies for each unique element of innovation. The purpose of this phase or step is to move the outcome to a measurable success. For innovation project success, there remains the issue of good project management. Without these critical resources, plans and strategies will fail. Of course, on the other hand, using only good project planning skills will not achieve instant innovation success. You must have a strategy as well; when used with established project planning and execution tools, ENOVALE Strategies will greatly increase success.

Discussion Questions

1. What step in the ENOVALE Strategies process would be (1) simplest and (2) most difficult for your organization?
    a. What would enhance success?
    b. What barriers exist?
2. Why are outcomes so critical for these strategies to work well?
3. Has your organization struggled with change?
    a. Were the benefits always positive?
    b. Do negative results resonate within the organization?
        i. Is this a process or people issue?
        ii. Was a decision made in haste or without review and evaluation?
4. Does the organization rely on a single point or integrated measurements?
    a. Can process or product measurements fail to signal potential problems?
    b. Were opportunities lost due to the inability to identify and track these measures?

Chapter 13

Achieving Success

Introduction

ENOVALE® Solutions transforms an organization with the necessary elements for managing an innovation project to success. It differs greatly from a traditional approach, where projects such as these were the responsibility of a small group of individuals. In fact, the people we talk to tell us that innovation is important; they are just not sure how to do it! They are searching for the methodology that you now have.

ENOVALE Solutions works with any organization (nonprofit, government, or traditional business). All organizations need this transformative process. Innovation is possible within any operation, function, or process. Outcomes change with each theme of innovation as well as measures of success applied. What remains the same is that innovation begins with a need and ends with the judgment of individuals. Innovation is one concept needed by all organizations. Our intention was to generalize innovation so that any organization can and receive the benefits it desires.

Think of a recent project that did not en_ tory solution. Carefully consider each of the Minimizing or missing steps results in a decre for success—not for lack of creativity, but rather for lack of a process designed specifically for innovation projects. Skipping steps may seem reasonable, but each step builds upon the findings and learning of the previous step. Think of the information lost at each step and how this affects overall success.

We believe you can understand the problems—and the reasons for delays. We expect that you understand the wisdom in conducting a project following the ENOVALE Solutions process. Think of other ideas that led to failed projects. Was there another method that would have guided the organization to success?

Some people may wonder if they can apply the deliverables of the ENOVALE process to initiate an internal project, using traditional project management guidelines, reasoning, and software. Certainly, a well defined outcome, validated metrics, aligned team members, and assurances of project viability (feasibility) and sustainability provide an excellent set of deliverables to the project team. Traditional project management, at this point, provides a framework to conduct and manage the project. Elements of ENOVALE Strategies complement project management approaches and also enhance the chance of success.

Innovation projects are much more similar to building a new home than to a home improvement project. The amount of unplanned (unforeseen) events causes the most delays, the largest outlay of expenses, and the best chance for failure. With ENOVALE Strategies, you plan for negative consequences, and you develop alternatives. Planning for innovation is different from planning for traditional projects. The difference lies in the fact that experience and past judgments are not necessarily the best tools for prediction. Therefore, you develop contingency plans to detect, react, and adjust accordingly. As a wise person said, "It's what you don't know that can hurt you!"

We have provided information on how to conduct
ccessful innovation project. We did this by first adjusting
lefinition of innovation. We clearly stated that our research

confirmed this new definition and that it varies greatly among different cultures, generations, and job functions. The fact that it varies is not a problem, but an opportunity! You can choose the best person for the innovation project by determining who best understands the concept. This is truly a novel approach.

Once you select the right people, the next step is to convert the objective to an outcome. "Why the extra effort?" you ask. An objective is merely an event bounded by some period. An outcome is an objective plus its requirements (how it functions and what its use is). The additional information provides a better set of criteria for deciding the project's fate. If an innovation cannot perform to its requirements or lacks "fitness for use," then its chances of success are limited. Why not pull the plug at that point, prior to spending excessive funds? Without the benefit of ENOVALE Solutions, most innovation projects require large expenditures of cash, time, and resources before project cancellation.

Our long years of travel and consulting have shown us the need for validation. Validating what we expect to occur is a great predictor of what will occur. A large part of validation is risk assessment. You cannot predict future events without understanding the concept of risk and variation (volatility). Watching the stock market and selectively buying stocks requires a good understanding of risk and volatility. As Kenny Rogers sang, "You got to know when to hold them and know when to fold them." The same is true for innovation projects. Risk depends upon the amount of knowledge and experience you have; volatility depends upon those events outside your control. Now, we are not stock market experts, gurus, or pundits. We understand innovation, and we validate to minimize risk and prepare for variation. With risk and variation come consequences and the need for alternatives. By doing so, you vastly increase chances for success. This has been our combined experience of more than 50 years.

The next step or phase (as certain steps can run in parallel) is alignment and adaptation. It is not enough to align the expectations of team members (remember our organic view of innovation), but you must adapt people, process, and product (technology) for innovation success. The adaptation is one that prepares the organization for the innovation. We have seen numerous innovations (great ideas with a true market focus) that failed because the organization was ill prepared to manufacture the product due to present process capabilities and/or lack of available resources. This is what we mean by the word adaptation. Do not assume that your systems can handle innovation in its three-dimensional definitions. Plan, but be ready to adapt quickly, and success will follow.

As with any project, a good set of performance metrics is essential. Most people understand financial measures, but they poorly understood the measures of nonfinancial performance. If the driving mechanism is the cost (or profit), the organization greatly increases the risk of failure. Why? Because performance is what the customer or user evaluates after cost. If the product, process, or employees fail to perform, the consequences will be painful and costly. Planning helps tremendously, but measuring performance and linking it to innovation is a key to success.

Finally, the project can begin now that all the preparations are in place. The execute phase is one that brings the outcome, the aligned team, the validated requirements, and the adaptable team together and links them with measures of performance. These preparations ensure further success, even if a traditional project management approach is used. When they are combined with ENOVALE Strategies, project success is ensured. Will all projects be successful? No, but a large percentage (70%) will achieve their original objectives. How can we say this? Our experience and actual demonstrated success prove this to be true. A true commitment and understanding of innovation is necessary for success.

The responsibility for sustained innovation lies with management. Innovation is not something someone can dictate or demand. It is not a one-person position; it requires many people aligned to a series of outcomes. Integrating innovation into an organization is a gradual, systematic approach, with each project creating a set of new learning and small successes. The organization learns how to use innovation for specific gain and does not confuse it with operational goals and objectives. Customers and end users should see the gains and realize that the provider is meeting more of their needs. One method that highlights the commitment that organizations make to innovation is that of certification.

Certification

It may seem that the goal to be innovative is open only to larger companies with greater resources. How can a small business innovate when employees and management are concerned with survival and day-to-day growth? Is it possible to certify an organization rather than individuals? Can organizations demonstrate the skills and practical understanding to be innovative? The answer is a resounding "yes" to all these questions. What it takes is a commitment to an innovation management process and a strategy that sustains innovation. It takes a commitment to the ENOVALE process and the skills to conduct a project that demonstrates successful implementation.

Certification is a viable option for small- to medium-sized businesses or organizations. We created a program, operated through the Project Impact Institute—Center for Innovation Excellence, to certify small- and medium-sized companies as innovators. This certification enables such organizations to compete with larger firms. The certification process is one that ensures that the organization understands innovation, has developed an innovation management process, can apply it to a specific need, and is dedicated to sustaining innovation. The purpose of the certification is to identify such organizations, enabling organizations to compete in an ever crowded marketplace.

In general, the organization commits a small number of employees (so small that the number could be one employee) to an overall assessment of the organization's preparedness, 4 days of training, and completion (and approval) of an innovation project. Certified organizations demonstrate their understanding of innovation through project success and commitment to innovation as an organizational (corporate) strategy. Visit the Global Targeting, Inc. website (www.globaltargeting.com) for more information.

Long-Term Commitment

As with any new strategy, innovation requires long-term commitment. It is not about project successes, training, or the expertise of the workforce. It is about a committed effort to institutionalizing innovation throughout the organization. If you truly believe that innovation begins and ends with the individual, then involving individuals is the key to success. Their involvement should be throughout the organization. As much as the organization may need innovative products or services, it needs innovation in all areas (functions) of the organization. The Human Resources Department needs innovative processes and procedures as much as Research and Development does.

One reason why we discussed the idea of innovative change is that it directly affects employees. Individuals recognize innovation when it meets a new or unfulfilled need. How often have you felt the need to apply innovation to a process or procedure that affects employees? Meeting internal needs is often as critical as meeting external needs. It must be part of the overall organizational commitment.

Discussing long-term commitments at this stage may be a bit premature. Yet, using innovation for project success is a bit shortsighted. We recommend that you focus on achieving success but also on institutionalizing innovation as a long-term strategy. This long-term commitment will be the greatest challenge among those who understand innovation as a chance event.

Summary

This short book has provided you, the reader, with the tools and strategies to make any innovation successful. The purpose for this book is not only to describe the transformative ENOVALE Solutions process but also to begin the process of institutionalizing innovation as a more common rather than special event. Initiating and deploying innovation helps the organization to remain competitive in today's marketplace. Competitors will find it difficult to match the success of innovation and to provide the customer with a new or better product, process, or service.

The most revolutionary aspect of our research and experience is that innovative change is possible. Rather than a focus on product, process, or technology, change is the result of a specific decision. People make decisions and people initiate innovations. There is a true symbiotic relationship between the decision outcome and its perceived success or failure. Decisions created in an innovative environment result in perceptions that are positive, or at least neutral—even with negative consequences. Innovative change is positive since its benefits and consequences provide lasting value to the organization. Implementing this type of innovation will align individuals and change their expectations to expecting that changes initiated benefit the organization. Employees may not all agree with the decision, but they will understand the specific reasons for this decision and be better prepared to handle the consequences.

You now have the tools for success. What remains is the commitment to implement. We could have told you that it was simple and easy, but we assume that our readers are already aware of the complexity involved with innovation. We continue to receive e-mails, newsletters, and news reports of how innovation will propel a company or country into the twenty-first century. Oh, that it would be that easy! From this short book, you have learned that it takes commitment, resources, and a management strategy to succeed. You cannot buy the software that will magically produce multiple innovations. It begins and ends with the individual.

Finally, we have two requests of our readers. First, review an innovation project (assuming that it was a viable idea) that failed. Consider each step of the ENOVALE process; determine if failure occurred at that step or from a combination of steps. We guarantee that you will find the assessment helpful, if not enlightening. Second, apply one or more ENOVALE steps to your next project. Evaluate the result; we believe you will be surprised. Do not expect a miracle with just one step because that will not happen. What you will find is a new way to evaluate projects that are not dependent upon emotion, opinion, or chance. It is your choice. Let us know; we welcome all inquires about the process.

References

Baregheh, A., J. Rowley, and S. Sambrook. 2009. Towards a multidisciplinary definition of innovation. *Management Decision* 47 (8): 1323–1339.

Bing dictionary. n.d. Wheel. Retrieved from http://www.bing.com/search?q=wheel+definition&qs=AS&form=QBRE&pq=wheel+definition&sc=4-16&sp=1&sk

Caraballo, E., T. Bynum, and G. McLaughlin. 2011. How to foster innovation in BPO. *Globalization Today,* July–August: 28–33.

Caraballo, E., and G. McLaughlin. 2012. Perceptions of innovation: A multi-dimensional construct. *Journal of Business & Economics Research* 10 (10): 1–16.

Dahl, A., J. Lawrence, and J. Pierce. 2011. Building an innovation community. *Research–Technology Management,* September–October: 19–27.

Ferris, D., and S. Goldsmith. 2012, July 24. *The S&A Digest,* Baltimore, MD: Stansberry & Associates Investment Research.

Goksoy, A., B. Ozsoy, and O. Vayvay. 2012. Business process reengineering: Strategic tool for managing organizational change; an application in a multinational company. *International Journal of Business and Management* 7 (7): 89–112.

Golanz, S., and C. R. Bowen. 2011. Meeting employee requirements. *Industrial Engineer,* October: 45–48.

Keller, S., and C. Aiken. 2009. The inconvenient truth about change management. *McKinsey Quarterly* 1–18.

McLaughlin, G. 2012, June 25. Why is innovation so often hit or miss? *Innovation Management.* Retrieved from http://www.innovationmanagement.se/

Preziosi, R. C., H. McLaughlin, and G. McLaughlin. 2004. The relationship of learning orientation to organizational performance. *Journal of Business and Economics Research* 2 (4): 9–16.

Zhuang, L. 1995. Bridging the gap between technology and business strategy: A pilot study on the innovation process. *Management Decision* 33 (8): 13–19.

Zhuang, L., D. Williamson, and M. Carter. 1999. Innovate or liquidate—Are all organizations convinced? A two-phased study into the innovation process. *Management Decision* 37 (1): 57–71.

Index

About the Authors

Ervin L. "Vinny" Caraballo is the CEO of Global Targeting, Inc., a management advisory firm with a focus on helping companies expand and improve operations through global business development and sourcing strategy, as well as applying innovation methodologies to build a competitive advantage. He developed his expertise and honed his skills through senior management positions at several global technology and consulting firms and involvement in entrepreneurial ventures. Consequently, he has advised clients in the United States, Latin America, and Asia. Prior to entering the private sector, he served as a U.S. Army aviation officer.

As a scholar–practitioner, he has brought his management expertise and experience into the classroom as a professor of marketing, strategy, global operations, and supply chain management at numerous universities around the world. His interest in innovation research led him to create the Project Impact Institute, a global research and innovation certification-based organization that studies how culture impacts innovation. He has a doctorate in international business administration from Nova Southeastern University and an MBA from Webster University.

Greg McLaughlin is senior vice president, research and development, at Global Targeting, Inc. Greg brings a broad set of research and practical expertise on innovation strategy, deployment, and ongoing success. Greg's most distinguished skill is his ability to interpret data and provide a common sense, practical application. He can look beyond the numbers to find a solution to complex problems. Greg can convert

these findings into a usable set of information, whether it is in print or in conversation. His unique contribution to Global Targeting, Inc. has been the creation of the training materials and application of the ENOVALE methodologies. Greg can explain these integrated processes so thoroughly that it seems second nature to most individuals.

As an analyst, a researcher, and a technology executive, Greg has helped design and develop innovative products, processes, and systems. His career has enabled him to work on such critical innovative projects as digital photography, unique consumer products, high-tech aircraft materials and design, redesigned medical devices, and software development. Cost savings alone from these projects exceed $300 million. He honed his skills as a senior Six Sigma master black belt and quality management consultant, working directly with Dr. W. Edwards Deming.

Greg has held a number of executive positions with such organizations as Reynolds Metals Company, Inthesis, Inc., and ADT Security Systems. He has international business advisory and instructional experience. He has authored numerous publications and training manuals, including the book *Total Quality in Research and Development.*

His educational achievements include a doctorate in business administration from Nova Southeastern University and a master of science degree in statistics and an undergraduate degree in meteorology from the Florida

State University. Greg was director of doctoral research at Nova Southeastern University and was instrumental in creating an innovative dissertation and course room process for the doctor of business administration degree at Capella University.